Stage Rigging Handbook
Second Edition

Jay O. Glerum

Southern Illinois University Press

Carbondale and Edwardsville

01 00 99 98   5 4 3 2

Library of Congress Cataloging-in-Publication Data

Glerum, Jay O.
    Stage rigging handbook / Jay O. Glerum.—2d ed.
        p.   cm.
    Includes bibliographical references.
    1. Stage machinery—Handbooks, manuals, etc.   2. Stage
management—Handbooks, manuals, etc.   3. Theaters—Safety
measures—Handbooks, manuals, etc.   4. Theaters—Stage-setting
and scenery—Handbooks, manuals, etc.   I.Title.
PN2091.M3G54   1997
792′ .025—dc20   96-7589
    ISBN 0-8093-1744-3   CIP

The paper used in this publication meets the minimum requirements of
American National Standard for Information Sciences—Permanence of
Paper for Printed Library Materials, ANSI Z39.48-1984. ⊗

Contents

Preface to the Second Edition

In the last twenty years, stage scenery has changed noticeably with steel being used as a common building material and hard covering replacing muslin on flats. Movement of scenery can be exceedingly complex as directors and designers at all levels of the entertainment industry strive to create new techniques and production modes. With the dynamics of moving heavier scenery, added strain is placed on building structures and rigging systems. The technology used in such shows as *Starlight Express, Phantom of the Opera*, and *Siegfried and Roy* requires an understanding of physics and engineering to the extent that some production companies hire structural engineers to assist in modifying the venue and to design the structure of the scenery.

With increased magnitudes of loads and complexity of movement comes greater risk, as well as greater possibility, for injury. The courts have found facility owners, managers, supervisors, and riggers to be responsible for the maintenance and proper use of their rigging equipment and for providing adequate training of those who use it. Gathering a group of stagehands around the hemp lines to all pull together is no longer sufficient. Technology has progressed beyond that point.

This book is not a course in engineering. It is intended to help you understand theatrical rigging equipment, how to inspect and maintain it, and how to use it. It is your responsibility to use the equipment safely; and when the complexity of a rigging problem is beyond your expertise, it is your responsibility to find a reliable source to help solve the problem. Just as no single stage technician could possibly be expected to have the breadth and depth of knowledge required to understand all of the intricacies of people flying and stage, arena, outdoor, convention center, and ballroom rigging, neither does this handbook. It is a resource that touches on the scope of our profession but does not exhaust it.

The second edition of *Stage Rigging Handbook* includes two new parts. The first is an expanded discussion of the forces and loads on stage rigging components and the structure supporting them. The second is devoted to block and tackle rigging. Both of these parts are intended to increase your understanding of the equipment you use. The remaining four parts contain many minor revisions that have come about from written comments from readers and feedback from the rigging master classes that have been held since the first edition was printed. This edition does not include the "Recommended Guidelines for Stage Machinery and Stage Rigging" that constituted the appendix of the first edition. At the time of this printing, the United States Institute for Theatre Technology and the Entertainment Services and Technology Association are in the process of writing standards to replace the recommended guidelines. And as in the first edition, the information on applying wire-rope clips, now in section 6.02.C-1, is adapted from the *Wire Rope Users Manual*, 2d ed., Copyright © 1981 by American Iron and Steel Institute, and is used courtesy of the American Iron and Steel Institute.

Beyond the acknowledgments contained in the original preface, some additional thanks are due. I owe a debt of gratitude to Randy Davidson for organizing the first master classes and to David Lofton and Jerry Gorrell for making them happen. From the teachers in the classes I learned much: Bob Beebe, Wally Blount, Randy Davidson, Harry Donovan, Peter Foy, Steve Langley, Randy Longerich, Rocky Paulson, and Mike Wheeler. Thanks also go to all of the participants who shared with me their knowledge of rigging. Special thanks are due to Rocky Paulson and John Burgess for critiquing early drafts of part 1. Credit is due to Harry Donovan for algebraically deriving the formulas for hanging points of unequal heights in section 1.05.E.

Thanks to Teresa White of Southern Illinois University Press for shepherding the manuscript to its finished form and Kathryn Koldehoff for her meticulous copyediting. As with the first edition, my wife, Sallie, spent hours editing and commenting on the work in progress. This book could never have happened without her.

Preface to the First Edition

The single greatest cause of rigging accidents in the American theatre is operator error. While some of this error is due to carelessness, much of it is due to lack of knowledge about rigging systems and their safe operation.

Stage Rigging Handbook is intended as a source of written information on the care and safe use of stage rigging equipment. It is hoped that its availability will help to reduce operator error–related accidents, thereby making the theatre a safer place to work.

This book could not have been written without the knowledge so generously shared by the people with whom I have worked.

I wish to thank Charlie Ford and Jim Waring of Catholic University; Warren "Tyke" Lounsbury, John Ashby Conway, and the late Lance Davis of the University of Washington; Floyd Hart and the stagehands of Local 15, IATSE in Seattle; the stagehands of Local 18, IATSE in Milwaukee; and all the road crews with whom I worked over the years.

I would also like to thank my colleagues in the stage rigging industry, especially those at the Peter Albrecht Corporation: Paul Birkle, President; the engineers and staff members.

The words could never have been put into print without the understanding, encouragement, and help of my family, particularly my wife, Sallie.

For permission to quote from the *Wire Rope Users Manual*, 2d ed., I thank the American Iron and Steel Institute. I also thank the United States Institute for Theatre Technology for allowing me to reprint their *Recommended Guidelines for Stage Rigging and Stage Machinery Specifications and Practices*. For permission to reproduce a number of the illustrations, I gratefully acknowledge the Peter Albrecht Corporation, the Macwhyte Corporation, and the American Iron and Steel Institute. And for illustration reproduction, I thank Wes Jenkins.

Symbols and Abbreviations

$\angle$ = angle
" = inch
' = foot
° = degree
$\searrow\uparrow$ etc. = a force
Σ = summation
$a, b, c \ldots$ = values
A = area
AF = applied force
AL = allowable load
ALL = allowable load limit
D = distance
D = sheave diameter
d = rope diameter
DF = design factor
D_F = free-fall distance
D_S = stopping distance
e = strain
FA = fleet angle
ft-lb = foot-pound
H = horizontal force
HF = horizontal tension force
in-lb = inch-pound
kip = kilopound
kip-ft = kilopound-foot
kN = kilonewton
L = length
L = load
l = left
l = change in length
lb/ft = pound per foot
lb = pound
lb-ft = pound-foot
LIF = load increase factor
LL = lead line
LLP = lead line pull
M = moment
M = multiplier

MA = mechanical advantage
N = number
N = newton
N-m = newton-meter
P = point load force
R = ratio
r = radius
r = right
R = reactive force
RP = radial pressure
S = stress
S1, S2, etc. = support line
SRF = strength reduction factor
SWL = safe working load
T = tension
UBS = ultimate breaking strength
V = vertical force
VF = vertical tension force
W = weight
WLL = working load limit
x = multiplication
Y = yield point

Stage Rigging Handbook

Part 1   Loads and Reactions

1.01   The 4 K's

Rigging is a tool used in the theatre. It supports and provides movement of overhead objects that are part of a production. If it works as it should, it rarely calls attention to itself. If something goes wrong, it may not only be noticeable but life threatening as well. The functions of the rigging equipment and the rigger are to do the job as the designer designed it and the director directed it and to do it safely. In order to do that, there are 4 principles that a rigger needs to follow, called the *4 K's* of rigging.

1. Know the rigging system you are working with.
2. Know that it is in safe working order.
3. Know how to use it.
4. Keep your concentration.

Everything that follows in this book is an elaboration of these 4 principles.

1.02   Knowing the Rigging System

A typical rigging system is made up of individual line sets. The line sets may be hemp, counterweight, or motorized (or a combination). Each line set is made up of individual components, such as rope, a head block, loft blocks, and so on. Each line set is a separate subsystem, that is, a group of components interrelated and working together. Knowing the rigging system means knowing:

1. The capacity of the equipment. You must know how much weight each line set is designed to hold, the maximum speed that motorized line sets are designed to travel, the maximum weight that all of the line sets together can hold, and the maximum additional weight that the grid steel can support.

2. The capacity of the components. You should know the maximum load that each component is designed to carry. A 6-line counterweight set may be designed with a total capacity of 1,500 lb. The individual loft blocks may be designed to support only a load of 250 lb each. The head block support steel may or may not be designed to support all of the line sets at the full load of 1,500 lb each.

3. The operating characteristics of the system. Each line set is unique. It has its own sound and feel; it even has its own smell. In order to know the system, the rigger should know the individual peculiarities of each line set in the system. By knowing how a line set operates normally, the rigger can detect abnormal operation and possible problems.

A.   Load and Force

A part of *knowing the rigging system* is understanding the forces that an object places on each component of a rigging system and the structural members supporting the components. When an object—whether it is a piece of scenery, a lighting instrument, or an actor—is flown, it exerts a force on all of the elements that support it. Within the confines of this book, the *object* will be referred to as the *load*. The *elements* include all of the components of the rigging system and the structural members of the building supporting those rigging components. The term *force* can be thought of as a *strength or energy trying to cause motion or change.*

B. Static Equilibrium

Newton's third law of physics states that *for every action there is an equal and opposite reaction.* Applied to rigging, this means that the rigging components and supporting members resist the applied force of the load with a reactive force exactly equal and opposite to the applied force. For example, imagine yourself holding a cup of coffee. The muscles in your arm and hand apply only enough force to support the weight of the arm and the cup of coffee. If less force is applied, your arm bends down and the coffee spills. If more force is applied, the coffee is thrown up in the air. A lighting instrument is hung on a batten. If the light is steady and does not move, all of the supporting components—the C-clamp, batten, lift lines, loft blocks, loft block support steel, head block, head block beams, arbor, rope lock, and lock rail—are exerting exactly enough force to hold it in place.

Two distinct branches of mechanics, *statics* and *dynamics*, apply to stage rigging. *Statics* is the study of forces and the effect of forces acting on rigid bodies *at rest. Dynamics* deals with motion and the effect of forces acting on rigid bodies *in motion.* A *body* is any object or component that can be isolated and analyzed separately, and a *rigid body* is an object that essentially retains its shape. An examination of some of the principles of statics will help in understanding how the load affects the rigging components and the support members. When there is no movement of an object, it is in *static equilibrium.* There is a balance of all of the forces acting on the system. *The force law of equilibrium* states that *the algebraic sum of all forces acting on an object in static equilibrium is zero.* This means that all of the forces acting on the body are equal and opposite.

1.03   Supporting a Load

A.   The Engineer and the Rigger

The following discussion is for the purpose of helping riggers to become aware of the forces acting on rigging systems and components, to help you *know the rigging system* that is being used. It is not intended to be a course in structural or mechanical engineering. Of necessity, the information on forces and strength of materials is condensed. The structural design of a building and the mechanical design of a rigging component are both complex procedures and require the expertise of a professional engineer. When in doubt, consult one.

Until antigravity devices are perfected, the load and rigging components must be supported by something. Frequently that something is a beam made from steel, concrete, aluminum, or other material. Each of these materials has its own strength characteristics that enable it to resist applied forces. Strength of materials is discussed later, in section 1.06. First we look at exactly how applied and resultant forces act on supporting members.

B. Seat-of-the-Pants Experience

One common experience most people have with resultant forces is riding on a seesaw. This is a simple beam with a center pivot point, or fulcrum. Through tactile contact between the seat of the rigger and the seesaw, we have tangible experience with beam loading and the strength of the beam material. We know that it works best if both people are about the same weight. It is easier to balance and easier to operate. For purposes of this discussion, assume that the seesaw is not moving, that it is a perfectly balanced plank 16′ long supporting 2 riggers, each weighing 200 lb, sitting on the ends. The components of the system are a 16′ beam (the seesaw), a section of pipe (the fulcrum), and 2 pipe legs supporting the fulcrum.

C. Free Body Diagram

Analyzing the forces acting on a body can be quite complicated at times. A good technique to follow is to make a drawing of the object isolated, or free, from all of its support members, showing all of the applied and reactive forces acting on it. This type of diagram is called a *free body diagram* (FBD). Figure 1.1 is an example of using an FBD to show the forces acting on the seesaw beam.

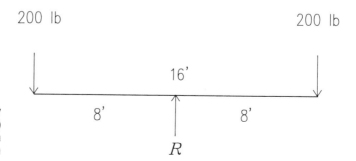

200 lb   200 lb

16′

1.1 Free body diagram (FBD) of forces on a seesaw beam

8′   8′

R

4

Forces are indicated by arrows. Reactive forces are indicated by the letter *R*. The diagram should contain the following information:

- The *length* of all supporting members and the distances between forces
- The *magnitude* of all of the known forces
- The *point of application* of all forces
- The *direction* of all of the forces
- The *sense* of all forces

The *length* of the supporting members is self-explanatory. The *magnitude* is the amount of force acting on the object. It can be expressed in units of

pound (lb)
1,000 lb, or a kilopound (kip)
2,000 lb, or a ton

Metric units are expressed in units of

newton (N)
1,000 N, or a kilonewton (kN)

The *point of application* is the place on the object where the force is being applied. The *direction* indicates the line of force at the point of application, such as an up and down direction. The *sense* indicates if the force is positive or negative, that is, up or down. Sometimes the sense is not obvious; this will become clearer in a later example.

D.   Summation of Forces

Earlier it was indicated that a body is in equilibrium when the algebraic sum of all the forces acting on it is zero. All forces have sense, and the following conventions will be used in this book. Forces up and to the right are positive. Forces down and to the left are negative (figure 1.2). The positive or negative direction of a force is its *sense*.

The symbol used to indicate sum, or summation, is the Greek capital letter sigma, Σ. When the forces acting on an object are in equilibrium, the equation can be written as follows: $\Sigma F = 0$. That is, the sum of all of the forces acting on the object equals zero. For purposes of analysis, it is usually necessary to determine all of the horizontal and vertical forces acting on an object. The equations for those forces are $\Sigma H = 0$ for the horizontal forces and $\Sigma V = 0$ for the vertical forces.

Ignoring the weight of the seesaw for the time being and labeling

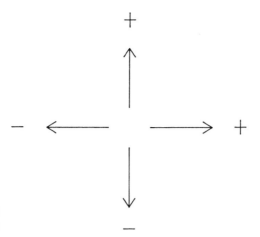

1.2 Positive and negative forces

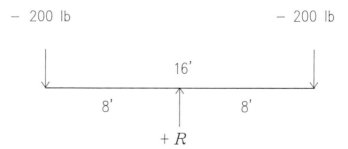

1.3 FBD with negative and positive forces

the forces in figure 1.3, there is a left (*l*) downward (thus negative) force of 200 lb, a right (*r*) negative force of 200 lb, and an unknown positive reaction. These are the vertical applied forces. There are no horizontal forces in this example. The symbol *P* indicates all applied point load forces, and the symbol *R* indicates all reactive forces. Using the equation we have:

$$\Sigma V = 0$$
$$\Sigma V = P_l + P_r + R$$
$$R + P_l + P_r = 0$$
$$R + -200 \text{ lb} + -200 \text{ lb} = 0$$
$$R = 400 \text{ lb}$$

The fulcrum is supporting a load of 400 lb and therefore must be reacting with a force of 400 lb.

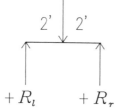

1.4 FBD of pipe legs

-400 lb

$2'$ | $2'$

$+R_l$ $+R_r$

This is only part of the problem. The pipe legs supporting the fulcrum still must be analyzed. Isolating the fulcrum in figure 1.4, the FBD shows the applied force on the fulcrum and the reactions of the pipe legs. The total applied load on the fulcrum is 400 lb: 200 lb for each rigger. Using the same formula:

$$\Sigma\ V = 0$$
$$\Sigma\ V = R_l + R_r + P$$
$$P = -400 \text{ lb}$$
$$R_l + R_r - 400 \text{ lb} = 0$$
$$R_l + R_r = 400 \text{ lb}$$
$$\text{Each } R = 200 \text{ lb}$$

When the beam is supported at each end and the load is in the center of the beam, the formula can be simplified to $V = P/2$, meaning the vertical reaction at each point is one-half the load.

E. Moment of Force

The *moment of force is the force's tendency to produce rotation of the object on which it acts. This rotation is about some axis or point of rotation.* The point of rotation is called *the center of moments,* and the distance between the applied force and the axis is called the *lever arm, or moment arm.* The length of the lever arm is measured from a line drawn through the axis perpendicular to the line of action of the force (figure 1.5). Units of measurement of a moment are expressed in distance and force, that is, inch-pound (in-lb), foot-pound (ft-lb), kilopound-foot (kip-ft), and newton-meter (N-m). (Sometimes the order of the units is reversed, such as pound-foot [lb-ft], but the meaning is the same.) In the seesaw example, figure 1.6, the seesaw is 16′ long. The fulcrum, or axis, is in the center, 8′ away from the applied force of the 200-lb rigger. To

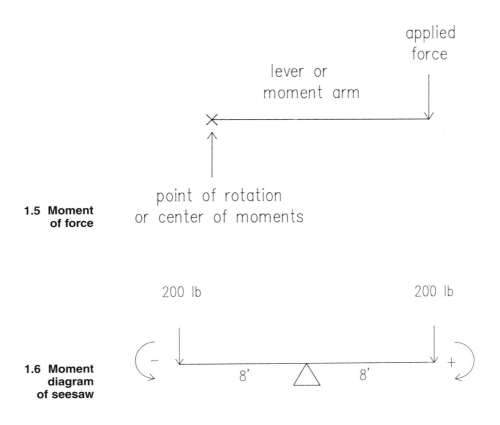

1.5 Moment of force

1.6 Moment diagram of seesaw

calculate the moment of force applied by a rigger, multiply the length of the lever arm (8′) by the weight of the rigger (200 lb). The result is 1,600 ft-lb.

The law of equilibrium applies to moments as well as to vertical and horizontal forces and is written $\Sigma M = 0$. Since the moment on the right end of the beam is 1,600 ft-lb in a clockwise direction, the moment on the left is also 1,600 ft-lb but in the counterclockwise direction. That is, the moments must be equal and opposite in direction. Think of it as clockwise being positive and counterclockwise being negative.

There are some seesaws that have movable pivot points on them. This is to accommodate people of unequal weights. By moving the beam off center, the length of the moment arm is changed and balance can be maintained. For example, if one rigger weighs 225 lb and the other weighs 175 lb, the distances (*D*) from the fulcrum would have to be adjusted to keep the seesaw balanced. Fig-

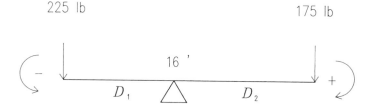

1.7 FBD of seesaw with unequal loads

ure 1.7 is an FBD showing the applied forces and the length of the beam. By simple addition, $\Sigma\, V = 0$, the reaction at the fulcrum is 400 lb. D_1 and D_2, the distances from the fulcrum to the applied loads, can be found by calculating, or "taking moments," from a point of rotation along the beam. Using the left end of the beam as the point, starting at the right end and taking moments of all of the forces acting on the beam, the moments are:

175 lb $\times$ 16′ = 2,800 ft-lb clockwise (+)
400 lb $\times$ D_1 = 2,800 ft-lb counterclockwise (−)
 225 lb $\times$ 0′ = 0

Because the moment is being taken at the left end, there is no length to the moment arm at the support point of the 225 lb.
  To find the length of the moment arm for the left side (the distance from the left end to the fulcrum), take the total moment of the right end and divide it by the force at the fulcrum.

$$\Sigma\, M = 0$$
$$\Sigma\, M = (D_1 \times 400\ \text{lb}) + (175\ \text{lb} \times 16')$$
$$(D_1 \times 400\ \text{lb}) + (175\ \text{lb} \times 16') = 0$$
$$D_1 = 2{,}800\ \text{ft-lb} \div 400\ \text{lb}$$
$$D_1 = 7'$$
$$D_1 + D_2 = 16'$$
$$D_2 = 16' - D_1$$
$$D_2 = 16' - 7'$$
$$D_2 = 9'$$

This can be checked by taking moments at the right end of the beam.

F. Examples

Three examples of using moments to calculate reactions on beam supports follow.

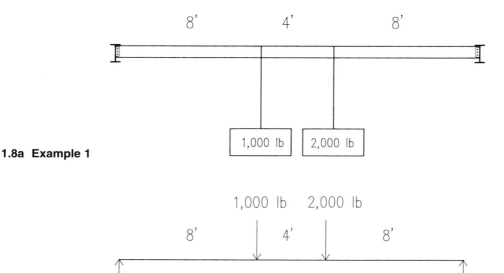

1.8a Example 1

1.8b FBD of figure 1.8a

R_l R_r

Example 1. Two rigging points are hung from a 20′ beam, as indicated in figure 1.8a. What are the reactions on the left and right support points? Constructing the FBD in figure 1.8b and taking moments at the right end:

$\Sigma M = 0$
$(R_l \times 20') + (-1,000 \text{ lb} \times 12') + (-2,000 \text{ lb} \times 8') = 0$
$(R_l \times 20') - 12,000 \text{ ft-lb} - 16,000 \text{ ft-lb} = 0$
$R_l = 28,000 \text{ ft-lb} \div 20'$
$R_l = 1,400 \text{ lb}$

Using $\Sigma V = 0$

$R_l + R_r - 1,000 \text{ lb} - 2,000 \text{ lb} = 0$
$R_r = -1,400 \text{ lb} + 1,000 \text{ lb} + 2,000 \text{ lb}$
$R_r = 1,600 \text{ lb}$

Example 2. The second example illustrates how to find the reactions for an evenly distributed load and includes the weight of the beam in the calculations. Up to now, we have ignored the self-

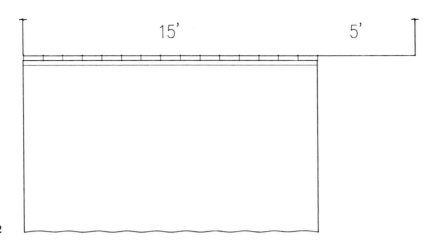

15' 5'

1.9a Example 2

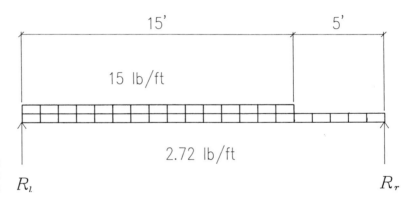

15' 5'

15 lb/ft

2.72 lb/ft

1.9b Weight distribution of figure 1.9a

R_l R_r

weight of the supporting beam. In practice, it must always be included in the calculations.

Figure 1.9a shows a 15'-wide curtain weighing 5 lb per linear foot (lb/ft), hung at one end of a 20'-long piece of 1½" schedule-40 pipe. The pipe is dead hung by rope at each end. How much weight does each rope support?

Weight of curtain = 5 lb/ft (75 lb total)
Weight of 1½" schedule-40 pipe = 2.72 lb/ft (54.4 lb total)

Figure 1.9b illustrates an FBD of the pipe and the evenly distributed loads.

Evenly distributed loads are calculated by adding up the total distributed load and assuming it to be a point load in the center of the

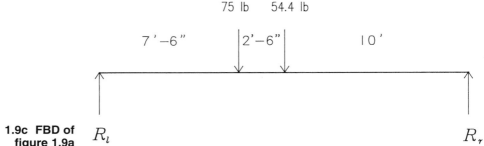

75 lb   54.4 lb

7'−6" |2'−6"| 10'

1.9c FBD of figure 1.9a R_l R_r

distributed span, as shown in figure 1.9c. Taking moments at the left end,

$\Sigma M = 0$
$(-75 \text{ lb} \times 7.5') + (-54.4 \text{ lb} \times 10') + (R_r \times 20') = 0$
$(R_r \times 20') = 562.5 \text{ ft-lb} + 544 \text{ ft-lb}$
$R_r = 1,106.5 \text{ ft-lb} \div 20'$
$R_r = 55.3 \text{ lb}$

$\Sigma V = 0$
$R_l - 75 \text{ lb} - 54.4 \text{ lb} + 55.3 \text{ lb} = 0$
$R_l = 74.1 \text{ lb}$

Example 3. The third example (figure 1.10a) illustrates the reactions of a wide-flange beam 10" deep, weighing 12 lb/ft (W10 × 12) overhanging a 5'-wide scaffold tower. A .5-ton chain hoist loaded to capacity is at the overhanging end of the beam. Determine the reactions at each of the support points of the beam (figure 1.10b).

$P = 1,000 \text{ lb}$
Weight of beam = $12 \times 12 \text{ lb} = 144 \text{ lb}$
Weight of chain hoist = 75 lb
Taking moments at R_l,
$\Sigma M = 0$
$(R_r \times 5') + (-144 \text{ lb} \times 6') + (-1,075 \text{ lb} \times 12') = 0$
$R_r = (864 \text{ ft-lb} + 12,900 \text{ ft-lb}) \div 5'$
$R_r = 2,753 \text{ lb}$

$\Sigma V = 0$
$\Sigma V = R_l + -144 \text{ lb} + -1,075 \text{ lb}$
$R_l = -2,753 \text{ lb} + 864 \text{ lb} + 1,075 \text{ lb}$
$R_l = -1,534 \text{ lb}$

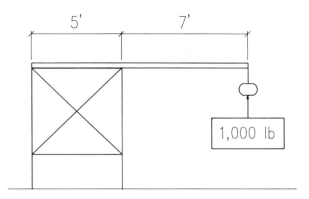

1.10a Example 3

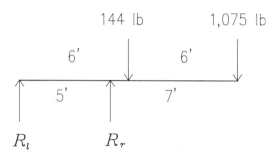

1.10b FBD of figure 1.10a

R_l R_r

In this case, the left reaction is negative, or a force in the down direction. There is a tendency for the beam to rotate with the fulcrum at R_r. A force of 1,534 lb on the left side, in the down direction, is necessary to keep the beam in equilibrium.

1.11 Continuous beam with 3 supports

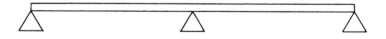

G. Continuous Beams

In the last section, there were several examples of beams supporting loads. In each of the cases, statics was used to calculate the reactions at the support points of the beam. Figure 1.11 illustrates a continuous beam with 3 or more supports. *Statics CANNOT be used to calculate the reactions if the beam has 3 or more supports.* A more complex method, called the *3-moment theorem*, is used for continuous beams. The 3-moment theorem is beyond the scope of this book but will be touched upon in section 3.04.A-2 on battens.

1.04　Summation of Forces

A.　Resultant Force

Figure 1.12a illustrates a 100-lb load suspended by a rope that is bent 360° around a pipe. Figure 1.12b is an FBD illustrating the forces at work in figure 1.12a. The load is 100 lb on the right side, and there is a 100-lb force on the left side holding the load in equilibrium. The sum of these 2 vertical forces is 200 lb in the down direction. The forces are acting on a common point, in this case the pipe, and the sum of the forces is called the *resultant force. The reaction is 200 lb in the up direction and is equal and opposite the resultant force. Two or more forces acting on a common point produce a single resultant force.*

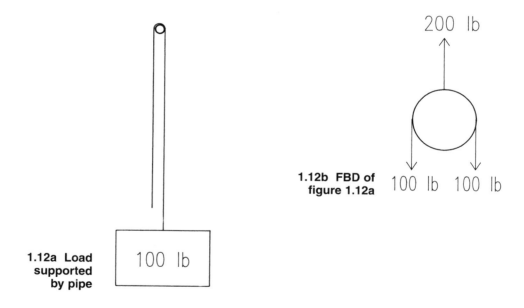

1.12a Load supported by pipe

1.12b FBD of figure 1.12a

Figure 1.13a depicts a line bent 90° around a pipe holding the same load. The FBD in figure 1.13b shows horizontal and vertical forces with 90° between the parts of the line. Intuition tells us that the pipe will tend to bend at a 45° angle between the parts of line. The magnitude of the force is unknown. When 2 equal forces in different directions act on a common point, the direction of the resultant force is halfway between the applied forces. This is true for the

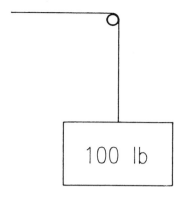

**1.13a Line bent
90° around pipe**

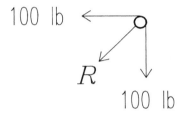

**1.13b FBD of
figure 1.13a**

example of the line bending around the pipe, a line going over a block, or a line bending around any point.

Figure 1.14 shows a line bent around a pipe at various angles. At 180° it is obvious that there is no load on the pipe. At 0° the resultant force is 200% of the applied load. As the angle between parts of line decreases from 180° to 0°, the resultant force increases from 0% to 200% of the load.

B.   The Law of Sines

Using a variation of the trigonometric law of sines, the resultant force can easily be calculated if the magnitude of the applied force and the angle between the parts of line are known. The formula to use is:

$F_r = P \times \sin \angle \div \sin \angle/2$

F_r = Resultant force
P = Applied force
$\angle$ = Angle between parts of line
$\angle/2$ = One-half of the angle between the parts of line

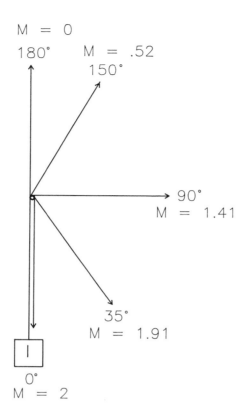

M = 0
180°   M = .52
          150°

90°
M = 1.41

35°
M = 1.91

**1.14 Line bent
around pipe
at various
angles, showing
multiplier (M)**

0°
M = 2

Figure 1.15 indicates a line supporting 100 lb bent 110° around a sheave. Using a calculator with trigonometric (trig.) functions, do the following:

Enter 110, sin (the sin of the included angle).
The calculator should read .93969 (the sin of 110°).
Enter ×, 100 (the load).
Enter ÷, 55, sin (the sin of ½ the included angle).
The calculator should read 114.71.
F_r is 114.71 lb or, rounded off, 115 lb.

C.   Table of Multipliers for Resultant Forces

Changing the load to 2,500 lb and using the same formula, F_r = 2,868 lb. Divide the resultant load by the applied load and round off: 2,868 ÷ 2,500 = 1.15. From the above example, dividing 115 lb by 100 lb equals 1.15. It becomes apparent that 1.15 is a multiplier

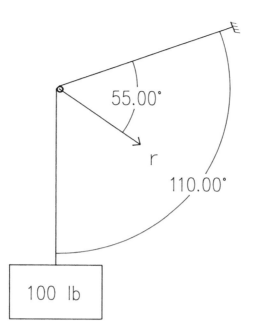

1.15 Line bent around pipe 110°

for 110°. To find the resultant force for any two forces separated by 110°, multiply the applied force by 1.15. The multipliers used to find the resultant forces for equal loads in increments of 5° are listed as follows:

Angle	Multiplier	Angle	Multiplier	Angle	Multiplier
180	0.00	120	1.00	60	1.73
175	0.09	115	1.07	55	1.77
170	0.17	110	1.15	50	1.81
165	0.26	105	1.21	45	1.85
160	0.35	100	1.30	40	1.88
155	0.43	95	1.36	35	1.91
150	0.52	90	1.41	30	1.93
145	0.60	85	1.47	25	1.95
140	0.68	80	1.53	20	1.97
135	0.77	75	1.59	15	1.98
130	0.85	70	1.64	10	1.99
125	0.92	65	1.69	0	2.00

Since the reaction is equal and opposite to the resultant force, this list gives the reactive force for the listed angles.

D. Vectors

Forces that have *magnitude, direction*, and *sense* can be drawn as vectors. Figure 1.16a is a *vector* drawing of the forces shown in figure 1.15. A scale is chosen to represent the magnitude of the force. In this case, each unit of length represents 10 lb of force. A line representing the magnitude and direction of each force is drawn to scale with an arrow indicating the sense of the force. The resultant force can be calculated by *geometrically* adding the vector forces. There are 2 ways to do this.

1. Parallelogram Method

Figure 1.16b illustrates a method whereby a parallelogram is constructed and the diagonal from the origin to the opposite corner is drawn. The diagonal represents the resultant force. If the vectors are carefully drawn, the length of the diagonal can be measured, and the resultant force can be closely approximated.

2. Tip-to-Tail Method

In the method shown in figure 1.16c, the vector for the vertical force is drawn starting at the origin. The diagonal force vector at 110° is drawn from the tip of the vertical vector. The resultant vector is drawn from the origin to the tip of the diagonal vector and measured. If a large enough scale is selected, and the drawing carefully done, the results can be very accurate.

1.05 Bridle Analysis

In section 1.04, it was shown that component forces can be combined to produce a resultant force. Often it is necessary to do the opposite and determine the horizontal and vertical components of a diagonal force.

Using bridles typically requires an analysis of the bridle components and the loads placed on all of the supporting members. The items that need to be calculated are the length of the bridle members; the force, or tension, on each bridle member; and the horizontal and vertical forces on each suspension point. Figure 1.17a shows a bridle being used to suspend a load from two support points. The given information includes the load and the horizontal and vertical distances of the load point from the hanging points.

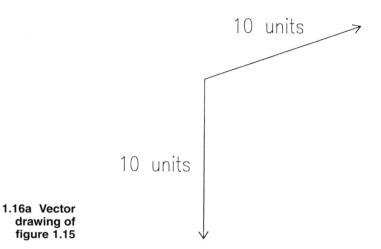

10 units

10 units

1.16a Vector drawing of figure 1.15

10 units

11.5 units

10 units

1.16b Completed vector drawing of figure 1.16a

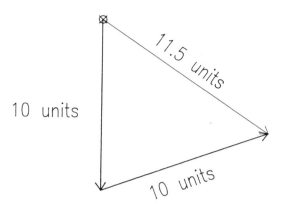

1.16c Tip-to-tail vector drawing of figure 1.16a

A. Bridle Length Calculation

If the horizontal and vertical distances from the hanging points are known, then calculating the required length of the bridle members can be done in 2 ways.

1. Scale Drawing

Carefully making a scale drawing of the bridle system and then measuring the length of the bridle members will give a close approximation of the required bridle length. If done on a computer-aided drafting (CAD) system, the results can be extremely accurate.

2. Pythagorean Theorem

The Pythagorean theorem can be used to find the length of the bridle legs mathematically. Figure 1.17b shows a right triangle with legs *a* and *b*. The theorem states that the square root of the sum of the squares of the sides is equal to the hypotenuse. Mathematically stated,

$$c = \sqrt{a^2 + b^2}$$
$$c = \sqrt{3^2 + 4^2}$$
$$c = \sqrt{9 \text{ sq ft} + 16 \text{ sq ft}}$$
$$c = \sqrt{25 \text{ sq ft}}$$
$$c = 5'$$

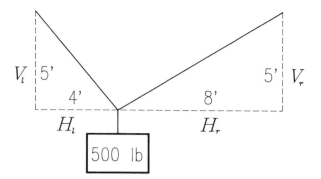

1.17a Bridle suspending load from 2 support points

Applying the formula to the bridle example shown in figure 1.17a, the length of the bridle members (L) can be calculated.

$$L_l = \sqrt{V_l^2 + H_l^2}$$
$$L_l = \sqrt{5^2 + 4^2}$$
$$L_l = \sqrt{25 \text{ sq ft} + 16 \text{ sq ft}}$$
$$L_l = \sqrt{41 \text{ sq ft}}$$
$$L_l = 6.4'$$

$$L_r = \sqrt{V_r^2 + H_r^2}$$
$$L_r = \sqrt{5^2 + 8^2}$$
$$L_r = \sqrt{25 \text{ sq ft} + 64 \text{ sq ft}}$$
$$L_r = \sqrt{89 \text{ sq ft}}$$
$$L_r = 9.4'$$

B.   Vertical and Horizontal Forces

All of the forces supporting the load must be in equilibrium. At this point in the bridle analysis, the length of the components and the weight of the load are known. The next step is to find the magnitude of the vertical and horizontal forces on each suspension point. Looking again at figure 1.17a, it is obvious that the total vertical force in the up direction must equal 500 lb. $\Sigma V = 0$. It is also obvi-

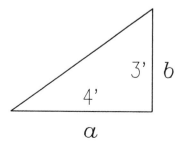

1.17b Right triangle

ous that there will be more load on the left suspension point than on the right because the load is closer to the left side.

1. Vertical Forces

As long as both hanging points are the same height, $V_l = V_r$, the moment formula, $\Sigma M = 0$, can be used. It makes no difference that the applied load is a vertical distance away from the support points. (See section 1.05.E for hanging points of different heights.) Taking moments at the left support point to solve for the vertical force *(VF)* at the right support point *(r)*, VF_r, we have:

$\Sigma M = 0$
$\Sigma M = (H_l \times P) + [(H_l + H_r) \times VF_r]$
$\Sigma M = (4' \times 500 \text{ lb}) + (12' \times VF_r)$
$(4' \times 500 \text{ lb}) + (12' \times VF_r) = 0$
$VF_r = 2{,}000 \text{ ft-lb} \div 12'$
$VF_r = 166.6 \text{ lb} = 167 \text{ lb}$

$\Sigma V = 0$
$\Sigma V = 500 \text{ lb} - 167 \text{ lb} - VF_l$
$VF_l = 500 \text{ lb} - 167 \text{ lb}$
$VF_l = 333 \text{ lb}$

2. Horizontal Forces

The horizontal forces must be equal to each other or the load will move from side to side: $\Sigma H = 0$. When the force in any one direc-

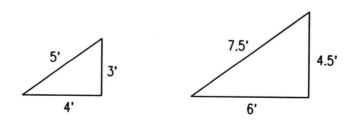

1.18 Similar triangles

$5/4 = 7.5/6 = 1.25$
$5/3 = 7.5/4.5 = 1.66$
$3/4 = 4.5/6 = .75$

tion on a bridle leg is known, and the horizontal and vertical distances of the bridle point from the suspension points are known, the other forces can be determined by using ratios of similar triangles. *When two triangles have the same angles but sides of different lengths, they are similar.* This means that the ratios of any two sides of one triangle will be equal to the ratio of the same two sides of the similar triangle (figure 1.18).

Figure 1.19a is the bridle diagram with the corresponding vertical force magnitudes shown. The diagram indicates the length of the bridle members and the distances the load is from the supporting points. It also indicates the direction and sense of the vertical forces. Figure 1.19b shows a vector drawing of the forces (in which *T* is the tension). Note that the legs of the triangles are of different lengths, but the angles are the same. Setting up the ratios to find the horizontal forces, we have:

$$5' \div 4' = 333 \text{ lb} \div HF_l \qquad 5' \div 8' = 167 \text{ lb} \div HF_r$$
$$HF_l = 4' \div 5' \times 333 \text{ lb} \qquad HF_r = 8' \div 5' \times 167 \text{ lb}$$
$$HF_l = 266 \text{ lb} \qquad HF_r = 267 \text{ lb}$$

The 1-lb difference is due to rounding off and is of no consequence; 267 lb is used for further calculations.

C.   Bridle Tension

The tension in the bridle leg can be calculated in several ways. Two of the methods are illustrated here.

1. Pythagorean Theorem

Using the Pythagorean theorem and the values for the horizontal and vertical forces, we have (after rounding off):

$$T_l = \sqrt{267^2 + 333^2} \qquad T_r = \sqrt{267^2 + 167^2}$$
$$T_l = 427 \text{ lb} \qquad T_r = 315 \text{ lb}$$

2. Comparative Ratio Method

$$4' \div 6.4' = T_l \div 267 \text{ lb} \qquad 8' \div 9.4' = T_r \div 267 \text{ lb}$$
$$T_l = 267 \text{ lb} \times 6.4'/4' \qquad T_r = 267 \text{ lb} \times 9.4'/8'$$
$$T_l = 427 \text{ lb} \qquad T_r = 314 \text{ lb}$$

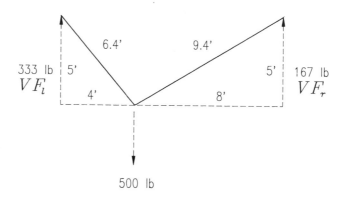

1.19a Bridle diagram showing vertical force magnitudes

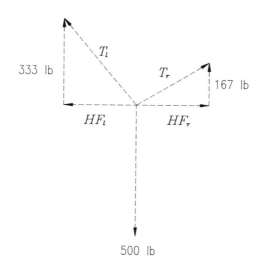

1.19b Vector drawing of figure 1.19a

D. Vector Analysis

Making a vector drawing for bridles is another way of solving for the vertical, horizontal, and bridle leg tensions. Use the original bridle drawing from figure 1.17a as a starting point. The horizontal forces acting on the bridle point are equal, therefore the horizontal components of the vector drawing are equal. Take the shortest horizontal component of the scale drawing, in this case H_l, and mark it off on the longest horizontal leg. Construct a new vertical, V_x, to intersect the bridle leg. Figure 1.20 shows the modified original drawing with the vector drawing superimposed.

The vector drawing is a scale drawing of the *forces* acting on the various elements of the bridle. While the drawing is accurate, the

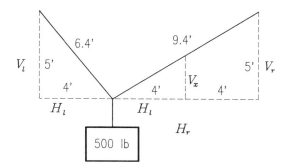

1.20 Partial vector drawing superimposed on figure 1.17a

scale, or value, of the units is unknown. Determine the length of V_x by using the ratio of similar triangles.

$$V_x \div H_l = V_r \div H_r$$
$$V_x = (V_r \times H_l) \div H_r$$
$$V_x = (5 \times 4) \div 8$$
$$V_x = 2.5$$

$\Sigma V = 0$; therefore the two vertical components in the *vector drawing* must equal 500 lb. Adding the number of units and dividing them into the weight gives us the weight-per-unit value of the vector drawing. 500 lb $\div$ (5 + 2.5) = 66.6 lb per unit. Now the force value of any component in the vector diagram can be found by multiplying the vector length by the unit value.

$$V_l = 5 \times 66.6 \text{ lb} = 333 \text{ lb}$$
$$V_x = 2.5 \times 66.6 \text{ lb} = 167 \text{ lb, and so on.}$$

E. Hanging Points of Different Heights

1. Vector Method

When the hanging points are of different heights, as in figure 1.21a, the bridle component lengths can still be calculated by the Pythagorean theorem, and the tension and forces can be calculated by the vector method in section 1.05.D. Figure 1.21b is constructed from figure 1.21a. The weight-per-unit value in the vector diagram is:

weight-per-unit = $P \div (V_l + V_x)$

(P is the point load force.) This is the sum of the vertical forces, or $\Sigma\ V = 0$. By similar triangles:

$$V_x \div H_l = V_r \div H_r$$
$$V_x = (V_r \times H_l) \div H_r$$
$$V_x = (6' \times 4') \div 8'$$
$$V_x = 3'$$

The weight-per-unit value is $500\ \text{lb} \div 8' = 62.5\ \text{lb/ft}$.

All of the forces can be calculated by multiplying the appropriate vector lengths by 62.5 lb. The left vertical force (VF_l) is:

$$VF_l = 62.5\ \text{lb} \times 5 = 312.5\ \text{lb}$$
$$VF_r = 62.5\ \text{lb} \times 3 = 187.5\ \text{lb}$$
$$T_l = 62.5\ \text{lb} \times 6.4 = 400\ \text{lb}$$
$$T_r = 62.5\ \text{lb} \times 5 = 312.5\ \text{lb}$$
$$HF_l = 62.5\ \text{lb} \times 4 = 250\ \text{lb}$$
$$HF_l = HF_r = 250\ \text{lb}$$

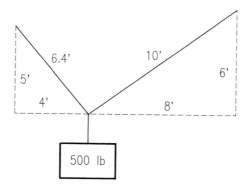

1.21a Bridle with hanging points of different heights

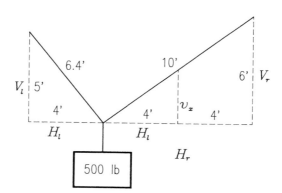

1.21b Partial vector drawing superimposed on figure 1.21a

26

2. Moment Method

If a vector diagram is not constructed and the value for the weight-per-unit is not found, the moment theorem, $\Sigma M = 0$, requires some modification for finding the vertical forces. The following section derives and illustrates the formulas.

$$VF_l = (V_l \times P) \div (V_l + V_x)$$

Without a vector diagram, the value for V_x is not known. Using the similar-triangle formula and substituting $(V_r \times H_l) \div H_r$ for V_x in the VF_l formula:

$$VF_l = (V_l \times P) \div [V_l + (\{V_r \times H_l\} \div H_r)]$$

To simplify the equation, both sides are multiplied by $H_r \div H_r$. (Note that $H_r \div H_r = 1$, so it does not change the VF_l side of the equation.)

$$VF_l = (V_l \times H_r \times P) \div [(V_l \times H_r) + (V_r \times H_l)]$$
$$VF_l = (5 \times 8 \times 500) \div [(5 \times 8) + (6 \times 4)]$$
$$VF_l = 312.5 \text{ lb}$$

Follow the same procedure for the other side:

$$VF_r = (V_r \times H_l \times P) \div [(V_l \times H_r) + (V_r \times H_l)]$$
$$VF_r = (6 \times 4 \times 500) \div [(5 \times 8) + (6 \times 4)]$$
$$VF_r = 187.5 \text{ lb}$$

The tension in the bridle legs can be found by similar triangles:

$$T_l \div VF_l = L_l \div V_l$$
$$T_l = (VF_l \times L_l) \div V_l$$

Substituting the VF_l formula from above for VF_l:

$$VF_l = (V_l \times H_r \times P) \div [(V_l \times H_r) + (V_r \times H_l)]$$

$$T_l = (L_l \times H_r \times P) \div [(V_l \times H_r) + (V_r \times H_l)]$$
$$T_l = (6.4 \times 8 \times 500) \div [(5 \times 8) + (4 \times 6)]$$
$$T_l = 400 \text{ lb}$$

Substituting the VF_r formula to find the tension in the right bridle leg:

$$T_r = (L_r \times H_l \times P) \div [(V_l \times H_r) + (V_r \times H_l)]$$
$$T_r = (10 \times 4 \times 500) \div [(5 \times 8) + (4 \times 6)]$$
$$T_r = 312.5 \text{ lb}$$

Summarizing the formulas:

$$VF_l = (V_l \times H_r \times P) \div [(V_l \times H_r) + (V_r \times H_l)]$$
$$VF_r = (V_r \times H_l \times P) \div [(V_l \times H_r) + (V_r \times H_l)]$$
$$T_l = (L_l \times H_r \times P) \div [(V_l \times H_r) + (V_r \times H_l)]$$
$$T_r = (L_r \times H_l \times P) \div [(V_l \times H_r) + (V_r \times H_l)]$$

F. Ratio of Horizontal to Vertical Distance

Changing the ratio of horizontal to vertical distance for the hanging points has an effect on the bridle tension and the horizontal forces on the hanging points. Figure 1.22 shows a series of bridles in which the vertical distance gets shorter in relationship to the horizontal distance. As the vertical angle approaches 90°, the tension in the bridle increases and the horizontal force on the hanging points increases. Assuming a 100-lb load, the vertical load on each hanging point is 50 lb. A comparison of the bridle tension and horizontal forces at various angles illustrates the increase in forces.

Angle	Bridle Tension	Horizontal Force
30°	58 lb	29 lb
45°	70 lb	50 lb
60°	100 lb	87 lb
80°	288 lb	284 lb
89°	2,865 lb	2,865 lb
89.9°	28,648 lb	28,648 lb

NOTE: When the angle between the bridle leg and the vertical is known, the following trigonometry formulas can be used: $T = VF \div \cos \theta$; $HF = T \sin \theta$.

The above comparisons show that, even though the supported load may be small, as the vertical distance decreases between the bridle point and the hanging points, the tension increases in the bridle. If too shallow a bridle angle is chosen, the tension in the bridle and the applied horizontal forces to the hanging points can be many times the load.

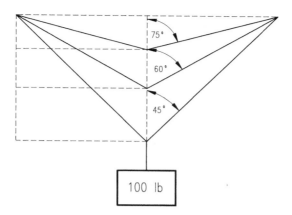

**1.22 Increasing
vertical angles**

G.   Allowable Loads

Sling manufacturers (a *sling* is just a bridle upside down) derate
the strength of their bridles as the angle between the sling leg and
the vertical changes. Since the tension increases in the sling member as the vertical angle approaches 90°, the sling will support less
weight. The sling member is given a working load rating based on
a straight vertical load. To find the allowable load of a bridle member at any angle, multiply the allowable load of the bridle member
by the cos of the vertical angle. The cos of 0° is 1 and therefore
can support the full load rating. The cos of 89° is .017. Due to the
increased tension in the member, at 89° the sling can support only
a small percentage of the load that it can support at 0°. If the rating
of a bridle member is 1,000 lb:

1,000 lb × cos 89° = allowable load
1,000 lb × .017 = 17 lb

Generally, the manufacturers want you to maintain a vertical angle of 45° or less.

H.   The Effect of Bridles on Hanging Points

When using a bridle, be sure that the hanging points can support
both the horizontal and the vertical forces of the bridle.

1. Separate Hanging Points

When the hanging points are separate, such as the individual
beams shown in figure 1.23, the beams must be braced in the horizontal direction to withstand the horizontal forces of the bridle.
While this principle may seem obvious to you, quite often no one

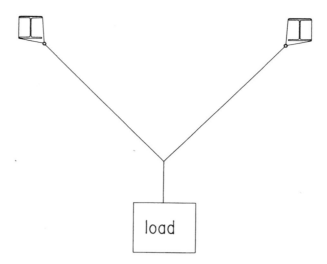

1.23 Hanging points on separate members

told the engineer who designed the beams that the supporting members would have to withstand these forces. Consequently, there may not be sufficient horizontal bracing. Imagine hanging a bridle from two separate battens with no stiffener between them. The horizontal force would pull the battens together. The same thing can happen to the beams in a building. Always calculate the horizontal, vertical, and tension loads on a bridle system before installing the bridle. Inspect the hanging points for horizontal bracing and any signs of deflection. (See 1.06.C for allowable deflection.) If there is no horizontal bracing, or if there is any question about the bracing being able to withstand the applied forces, have an engineer verify that the structure can support the load.

2. Hanging In-line on a Beam

Hanging the bridles in-line on a beam (figure 1.24) ensures that there is horizontal support. A batten is a simple beam, and bridling from it is a clear example of this type of hanging. There is a finite amount of weight that the batten, or any beam, can support in this manner. If the horizontal forces are too great, the beam will bend just like a bow when the string is drawn.

1.06　　Strength of Materials

The following discussion on strength of materials is brief and included to provide a foundation for understanding the terminology

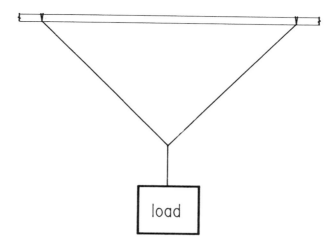

1.24 Hanging points on same member

that component manufacturers use in rating their products. There are some excellent books on the subject listed in the bibliography that do not require a degree in higher mathematics to understand. Not only are they very well written, some of them are even fun to read.

Every material that is used for stage rigging components and support members has a finite strength, a limited ability to resist the load placed on it. Generally speaking, the manufacturers of components tell the users how much load a component made from a given material can support before failure. There are several ways that this information is conveyed, and understanding the terminology is part of the rigger's job.

A. Types of Applied Forces

There are 4 types of applied forces that affect materials. These are *tensile,* or stretching, forces; *compressive* forces; *shear* forces; and *torsional* forces. (Torsional forces are discussed in section 1.06.E.)

A *tensile force* attempts to pull the material apart. This is generally the type of force placed on rope, cable, bolts clamping 2 objects together, and the bottom chord of beams. Not all materials withstand tensile forces well (figure 1.25a).

Compressive forces tend to push the material together and cause it to bulge. Footings, the top chord of beams, bolts used as

tension

load

leveling legs on appliances, and walls are examples of objects that have to resist compressive forces (figure 1.25b).

A *shear force* is a sliding force. It tends to make 2 parts of an object try to slide against one another. A load on the pin of a shackle is an example of a shear force (figure 1.25c).

In each of these cases, the external force is attempting to deform the material, and the material is resisting the force through the molecular bond of atoms within that material. Some materials resist one type of force better than others. Steel resists both tensile and compressive forces fairly well. Concrete and Styrofoam resist compressive forces well, but by themselves they are almost useless in resisting tensile forces. Rope and cable withstand tensile forces but are ineffective when resisting compressive forces. Trying to move a load by pushing a rope is futile.

B. Stress, Strain, and Hooke's Law

Stress (S) is defined as the load per unit of cross-sectional area. It is found by dividing the point load forces (P) by the cross-sectional area (A) of the object being tested, that is, $S = P \div A$. If a steel rod 1" square is supporting a load of 1 ton in tension, the amount of stress on the rod is 2,000 lb per sq inch, $S = 2,000$ lb $\div$ 1".

This same principle is true for compressive forces. When a woman weighing 120 lb walks on a pair of high heels and each side of the heel is .5" long, the area of the heel is $.25"^2$ (.5" × .5" = $.25"^2$). The compressive stress on the area of the floor where she

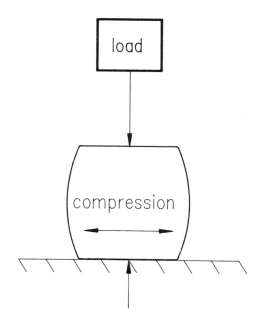

**1.25b
Compressive
force**

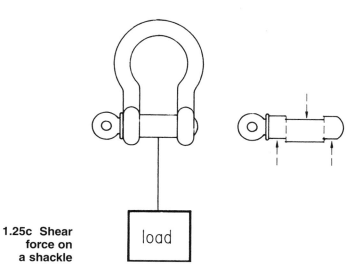

**1.25c Shear
force on
a shackle**

puts her heel at the moment when all of her weight is on that one heel is 120 lb ÷ .25" = 480 lb/inch^2. In tall buildings, as construction is completed, more and more material is added to the structure, increasing the weight that the building supports. The building compresses and actually gets shorter. Engineers must take this compression into consideration when designing the structure. Stress can be caused by either tensile or compressive forces.

In everyday life the terms *stress* and *strain* are used interchangeably: The stage manager is "stressed out." The technical director is under a lot of "strain." In the science of materials, stress and strain are very different. *Strain* is defined as the change in length of an object as force is applied to it. Strain (*e*) equals the change in length (*l*) divided by the original length (*L*) of the object, $e = l \div L$.

Robert Hooke was the first person to realize the relationship between stress and strain and write about it. His theory, Hooke's law, states that stress is directly related to strain. This is true for many materials, especially steel. When a piece of steel is subjected to a given load, either in compression or tension, it will change its length in proportion to the applied force. The steel rod with a cross-sectional area of 1 sq inch will stretch a certain length under a load of 1 ton. It will stretch exactly twice as much under a load of 2 tons. If the woman above weighed 240 lb, the floor would compress twice as much. Or, if the heel of her shoe had an area of only .125"^{2}, the floor would compress twice as much.

C. Yield Point and Elasticity

For many materials, when forces within a certain range are applied and then removed from an object, the object will go back to its original shape. These applied forces are within the *elastic range* of the material from which the object is made. If the amount of force is increased, it will reach a point where the object will not return to its original shape. This point is called the *yield point. At this point, the molecular structure of the material has been permanently altered.* An example of this is a rubber band that has been stretched to the point where it will no longer go back to its original shape. Common examples are a thimble that has been permanently deformed by stress (see figure 4.15) or a beam that is bent. The allowable deflection for a steel beam is 1/240 of the span between supporting points. A 20′-long beam supported at each end is allowed to deflect 1" in the center, a 10′ beam ½", and so on (figure 1.26a).

The yield point for a material is usually determined by laboratory testing. A sample of the material with a known cross-sectional area is subjected to carefully increasing forces, and the change in length is measured. This information is plotted on a standard stress-strain graph. Figure 1.26b is a typical stress-strain diagram for mild steel, the material from which structural and bar-stock steel components are usually made. As the stress induced by the load increases, the strain increases at a constant rate until it reaches the yield point.

If the force is released at any point of the test before the yield point is reached, the material will go back to its original shape. The force up to this point is within the *elastic range* of the material, and there is no change in the strength of the material.

At point *Y*, the yield point, the material stretches a greater distance than before in relation to the applied force. If the force is released at this point or any point beyond, the material will not return to its original shape. The molecular bond has been changed, and the elastic limit has been exceeded. Permanent deformation has

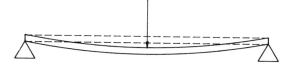

allowable deflection
. 1/240 of span

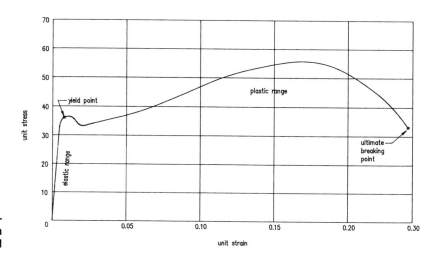

1.26a Allowable deflection for a steel beam

1.26b Stress-strain graph of mild steel

occurred, and the material is now in a *plastic* state. At this point, the material is no longer as strong as it was originally.

D. Ultimate Breaking Point

As increased force is applied to the material, it continues to stretch in a plastic state until it fails and breaks apart. This point is called the *ultimate breaking point*. Manufacturers often provide this figure as a rating for a given material. Some of the terms they use are *ultimate breaking strength, breaking strength, tensile strength, nominal breaking strength,* and *average breaking strength*. While these terms have slightly different meanings for the user, they are basically synonymous. When a component fails and breaks apart, the official terminology used in accident reports is that "the component suffered a catastrophic failure." Because the failure is usually accompanied by a loud noise, the riggers on the job will say that "the son of a bitch blew up." These two terms are also synonymous. "Catastrophic failure" equals "son of a bitch blew up." Whatever the term used, this result is to be avoided.

E. Torsion

A *torsional force* is a twisting force. Using a wrench to tighten a nut and bolt subjects the bolt to torsional force. The longer the wrench, the greater the force that can be applied. The strengths of the bolt and the nut must be able to withstand the force applied by the wrench or the bolt will fail. Most of us have, at one time or another, "over-torqued" a bolt and had that sinking feeling when it suddenly got easier to turn because the threads were stripped or the bolt broke apart. In both cases, the torsional force caused the material to fail in shear. *Shear*, as defined earlier, is 2 parts of the material sliding against one another. The torsional force that causes shearing is highly destructive and relatively easy for a person to apply to a component. It is impossible for any of us to pull a ¼"-diameter steel rod apart (tensile force) but relatively easy to strip a bolt of the same diameter if given a long enough wrench.

F. Unpredictable Forces

Tension, compression, shear, and torsion forces are fairly easy to predict and calculate under static conditions. Once the load starts

moving, the forces are increased and can be applied in unpredictable modes. Two of these modes are fatigue and shock loading.

1. Fatigue

Fatigue stress is caused by repeatedly applying and removing
force on an object. The force can be tensile, compressive, torsional, or any combination of the above. The components used for
rigging are all subject to dynamic loads and fluctuating stresses.
The actual stress can be well below the tensile strength or even
the yield point of the material.

Fatigue is progressive, hard to see, and very difficult to predict. If
a rigging system is designed for a single use with a constant load
and a constant number of cycles per time period, predicting fatigue
failure is possible. Most of the time, though, the loads and cycles
are changing and therefore unpredictable. Bending a paper clip
back and forth will eventually fatigue the piece of wire until it
breaks. That it *will* break is certain. *When* it will break is very
difficult to predict. Only regular inspection of the components can
tell when the fatigued parts are in danger of failing.

2. Shock Loads

The rapid application of force to an object is *shock loading*. It usually involves rapid acceleration or deceleration. Hitting the arbor on
the crash bar, a batten fouling on an adjacent batten and then falling free, or starting and stopping a motorized system are all examples of shock loading. The magnitude of shock load due to a free
fall can be approximated if the free-fall distance (D_F), the stopping
distance (D_S), and the weight (W) of the falling object are known.
The formula is:

Shock Load = $[(W \times D_F) \div D_S] + W$

On theatrical rigging systems, calculating the effect of a shock
load on specific components is extremely difficult. The stopping distance is dependent on the cross-sectional area, the length, the
coefficient of elasticity, and the percentage of load applied to each
component of the system.

G. Design Factor of Components, Working Load Limit

It is unsafe to place on rigging components loads equal to the
breaking strength or the yield point of the material. Usually a com-

ponent is given a *working load limit* (WLL) that is a percentage of the ultimate breaking strength of the material from which the component is made. Other synonymous terms for WLL are *allowable load limit* (ALL), *allowable working load* (AWL), *and safe working load* (SWL). *Safety factor* and *safe working load* are not the preferred terms because they imply safety, which may or may not exist.

The ratio of the allowable load to the ultimate breaking strength is called the *design factor* (DF) and is determined by dividing the *ultimate breaking strength* (UBS) by the *allowable load* (AL). As with any equation, this formula can be manipulated algebraically to solve for any of the 3 terms.

$$DF = UBS \div AL$$
$$AL = UBS \div DF$$
$$UBS = AL \times DF$$

H. Determining the Design Factor

The design factor provides a margin of safety for selecting and sizing rigging components. The question is, how large should the margin of safety be? The design factor, when not specified by a law, such as an Occupational Safety and Health Administration (OSHA) regulation, depends on the degree of risk involved in the situation. Dead hanging a 10-lb sack of feathers 8′ off the floor poses very little risk to anyone. If it falls, there is almost no chance of someone getting hurt or killed. The design factor for the suspension materials can be very low. Hanging a 200-lb chandelier on a single line that moves during an *a'vista* (in view of the audience) scene change over a stage full of actors has a much higher degree of risk. The design factor for all components should be increased to reflect the risk and provide an adequate margin of safety.

When calculating the design factor, every known force should be entered into the equation. A synonymous term for design factor is "*factor of ignorance*." This term is used by J. E. Gordon in his books on strength of materials and structures. The factor of ignorance implies that the design factor allows for all of the unknown forces. In addition to the load and the ultimate strength of the component, there are sometimes known factors that will increase the load, *load increase factors* (LIF). Typical load increase factors are the added weight that curtains gain by absorbing moisture from the air and the added force required to overcome the inertia of starting to move an object at rest.

There are also factors that will decrease the strength of the materials that are being used, *strength reduction factors* (SRF). Examples of strength reduction factors are a knot in a rope and the type of termination on a wire rope. These factors should be included in the calculations. The margin of safety provided by the design factor should allow for the unknown factors, such as shock loading and fatigue. The modified formula to include the strength reduction factors and the load increase factors is:

$$DF = (UBS \times SRF) \div (AL \times LIF)$$

The LIF is a multiplier including 100% of the load plus the increase percentage of the load.

$$LIF = 100\% + increase\ percentage$$

An LIF of 20% is expressed as 1.20 (100% load plus the increase).

The SRF is a percentage of the UBS. If a termination for wire rope is 90% efficient, then the UBS is 90% of the manufacturer's rating for the wire rope. An SRF of 90% is expressed in the equation as .90.

To determine the size of rope required to hang the chandelier in the above example, start with the known information and reasonable assumptions. The weight of the object and the efficiency of a bowline (60%) are known. A design factor of 10 is common practice for this kind of situation. Assume an added force of 10% of the chandelier's weight to overcome inertia and friction in starting and stopping the movement.

Weight of chandelier (AL)	200 lb
Required design factor (DF)	10
Efficiency of knot (SRF)	60%
Added force to overcome inertia (LIF)	10%

Modifying the formula to solve for the ultimate breaking strength of the rope with a design factor of 10, we have:

$$DF = (UBS \times SRF) \div (AL \times LIF)$$
$$UBS = (DF \times AL \times LIF) \div SRF$$
$$UBS = (10 \times 200\ lb \times 1.10) \div .60$$
$$UBS = 2,200\ lb \div .60$$
$$UBS = 3,667\ lb$$

Selecting a rope with an ultimate breaking strength of 3,667 lb provides a design factor of ten times all of the known forces. This allows a reasonable margin of safety for shock loading, fatigue, and any other unforeseen forces hidden in the factor of ignorance.

Part 2   Block and Tackle Rigging

2.01   Introduction

In section 1.01 the 4 main principles of rigging, called the 4 K's were introduced. In the following sections, these principles are applied to different kinds of rigging systems. The first section looks at their application to block and tackle rigging. We begin by getting to know the system. Under this heading, the things that the rigger needs to know to use a block and tackle safely are

1. The weight of the load to be lifted
2. The weight of the block and tackle
3. The capacity of the block and tackle
4. The *working load limit* (WLL) of the rope
5. The *lead line pull* (*LLP*)
6. The load capacity of the supporting member
7. The total load on the supporting member

2.02 Anatomy of a Block and Tackle System

A block and tackle consists of a *standing* (or *fled*) *block* attached to the supporting member, a *running* (or *fall*) *block* attached to the load, and a line of fiber rope (figure 2.1).

   The line for a block and tackle system can be natural or synthetic fiber. (More detailed information on types and strength of line is given later.)

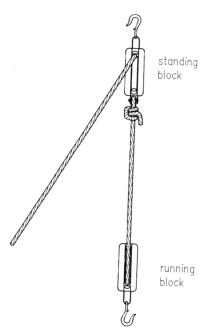

standing block

running block

2.1 Block and tackle

   The principal part of a block is the *pulley*, or *sheave*, consisting of one or more grooved wheels supported by wood or metal side plates that turn on a shaft. The block is used to change the direction of the force utilized to move an object with a line. It is much easier to raise something to the grid using a block and pulling down on the line than it is to stand on the grid and pull it up. Not only is there less strain on the back but the rigger can use body weight to help raise the load.

   Blocks are rated for working load limits. Each block should have a label on its side indicating the manufacturer's name and the working load limit. This rating indicates that all of the components of the block have been engineered to withstand the working load. Sometimes there is a code indicating the type of bearings used in the block. If the type of bearing is not evident, call the manufacturer to get a list of their codes. Do not use unrated blocks for heavy loads. If an unrated block fails while you are using it, it is your fault and you are liable.

A.   Wooden Blocks

Figure 2.2 shows the parts of a wooden block.

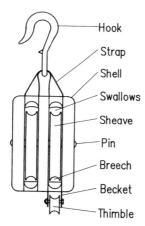

Hook
Strap
Shell
Swallows
Sheave
Pin
Breech
Becket
Thimble

2.2 Wooden block

1. The wooden shell (or cheeks) keeps the rope in the sheave groove.
2. The strap, made of steel, transmits the load from the pin to the hook.
3. The sheave, or pulley, is the grooved wheel over which the rope runs.
4. The pin is the axle on which the sheaves turn. The pin supports the entire weight of the load and transmits the load from the sheave to the straps.
5. The swallows is the larger opening through which the rope passes.
6. The breech is the smaller opening at the other end of the block.
7. The becket is the attachment point of the dead end of the line.
8. A thimble is used to reduce the stress on the rope at the becket.
9. A hook or shackle is used to attach the strap to a supporting member.

B. Metal Blocks

Metal blocks, figure 2.3, are similar to wooden blocks. If the metal shell (or cheek) is strong enough, it can actually support the pin and transmit the load from the pin to the hook, and no straps are needed. In addition, metal blocks very often have some type of improved bearing to allow the sheave to turn with less friction.

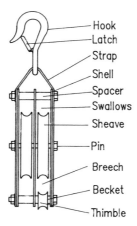

Hook
Latch
Strap
Shell
Spacer
Swallows
Sheave
Pin
Breech
Becket
Thimble

2.3 Metal block

C. Other Types of Blocks

Other types of rigging equipment are finding their way onto the stage. Venues close to navigable bodies of water sometimes use rated marine-grade sailing pulleys for block and tackle rigging. The blocks are load rated, lightweight, can be furnished with good ball bearings, and are easy to handle. Due to the small sheave diameter, they work particularly well with braided synthetic line.

For simple work lines, mountain-climbing rescue pulleys are easy to use. They are load rated, efficient, and lightweight.

2.03   Load Distribution on a Block

A. Static Load

Figure 2.4a shows a single block with a load of 100 lb on it. A force of 100 lb on the lead line is required to hold the load in static equilibrium. Recalling section 1.04.A, the resultant force on the block is 200 lb. There is also a force of 200 lb on the structural member supporting the block. When using a single block to support a load

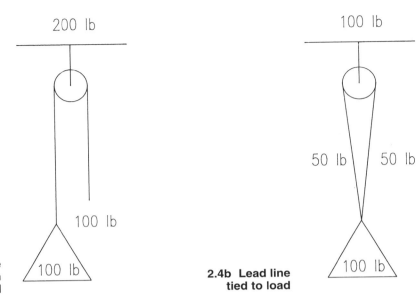

2.4a Single block with static load

200 lb

100 lb

100 lb

2.4b Lead line tied to load

100 lb

50 lb   50 lb

100 lb

with an angle between lines of 0°, the force on the block and the supporting member is doubled.

This type of rigging is commonly found in arenas and thrust theatres with dead-hung pipe grids. Scenic units, such as headers, are often hung from the grid. Block and tackle are used to raise the unit into position where it is dead hung with wire rope, piano wire, or some other "invisible" suspension medium. During the raising process, stagehands use single or multiple blocks to raise the unit to a working or trim height. The lead lines are often tied to the arms or legs of the auditorium seats to hold the header in position. Because seats are designed to withstand the downward load of a body, not upthrust, it is good practice to inspect the mounting bolts first to be sure that they are firmly attached to the floor, since tied off lead lines are exerting an upthrust on the seats.

In figure 2.4b, the lead line is tied off to the load instead of to the seat. By doing this, the load is distributed equally to both lines. Because half of the load (50 lb) is on each line, the load on the block and on the supporting member is only 100 lb. Untying the lead line from the load instantly doubles the load on the block and support.

The principle of distributing the load between 2 lines is used in many parts of stage rigging. One example is the difference in load distribution between a choker hitch and a basket hitch around a beam for arena rigging (figures 2.5a and 2.5b). The entire load is supported by one end of the cable in a choker hitch, while the load

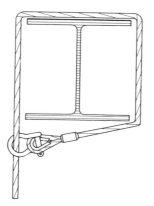

2.5a Choker hitch on a beam

2.5b Basket hitch on a beam

is split, with half on each side, in a basket hitch. A smaller-diameter wire rope can be used to support the same weight with a basket hitch. See section 4.05.D-1 for a similar example using trim chains.

Refer to figures 2.2 and 2.3 for the parts of a block. The entire resultant force is supported by the sheave, the pin, the attachment device, and the bearings. Half of the resultant load is supported by each side plate. Each of the components must be strong enough to do its job. If even one of them is not, the component will fail, and the load can fall.

B. Dynamic Load

1. Inertia

A body at rest tends to remain at rest, and a body in motion tends to remain in motion. This tendency to resist change in acceleration is called *inertia,* and it is the principle of Newton's first law of physics. We have experienced inertia when trying to push a car on a level road. (Usually it seems that cars must be pushed uphill, but that is a different problem.) More force is required to get the car rolling than to keep it rolling. A 100-lb load requires a force of 100 lb to hold it in position, but it requires more than 100 lb to move it. In addition to overcoming the friction in the system, moving the load requires enough force to overcome the inertia, that is, to change the acceleration from 0 to whatever speed we want it to move. With a block and tackle, we generally do not know the velocity that we want the load to travel. Therefore, an exact calculation of the inertial force is not practical. Even though inertia is not pragmatic to calculate, its existence causes an increase in the force required to move the load.

Once the load is moving at the desired speed, the inertial force is no longer needed. A force equal to the load, plus the force of friction, is required to keep it moving. There are 3 magnitudes of force on the block and supporting member: (1) the force of the load at rest; (2) the force required to accelerate the load to the running velocity, which is a force equal to the load plus inertial and friction forces; and (3) the force required to keep it moving, which includes the load force and the friction force. These changes in force are transmitted to the block parts, to the supporting member, and to the rope and cause fatigue in all of the parts of the system.

2. Friction

When asked to solve problems of force and movement in high school physics class, we were usually told to ignore friction. In real-life, ignoring friction is like ignoring the wind in a hurricane. Friction is always there. It is a real part of the system and it is extremely hard to calculate. There are 3 sources of friction in a block and tackle system. The first is the friction of the sheave turning on the bearings. Depending on the type of bearings and how well lubricated they are, the bearing friction can range from 1% to 10% of the load. Typical types of bearings used in block are

a. Common, or plain, bore. This is simply a hole drilled in the sheave for the metal shaft to rotate on, very common in wooden-sided blocks. This type of block has the highest friction factor and lubrication is always required.
b. Roller bearings.
c. Self-lubricating bronze bearings.
d. Pressure-lubricated bronze sleeves.
e. Ball bearings, usually found in boat pulleys and in some stage blocks.
f. Tapered roller bearings, found in some stage-loft and head blocks.

The friction factors for the various types of bearings are found in tables 2.1–2.4 in section 2.04.C.

The second source of friction is the rope. Regardless of the type of rope—synthetic, natural fiber, or wire—the strands and fibers rub against each other as they bend over the sheave. The smaller the diameter of the sheave, the sharper the bend in the rope and the more the fibers rub against one another. The recommended ratio of the sheave diameter to the rope diameter is discussed in section 3.03.G-9. The amount of lubricant on the rope fibers and the amount of moisture in a fiber rope also affect friction. It is not practical to calculate rope friction, but be aware that it exists and requires force to overcome.

The third source of friction results when lines are twisted (see section 2.05). Additional friction can occur if the line is oversized for the sheaves and rubs on the side plates. Also, if the blocks tilt, the line can rub on the side plates and cause additional friction.

2.04   Mechanical Advantage

Mechanical advantage is the ratio, or comparison, between the force required to move a load and the force of the load. The formula is:

Mechanical Advantage (MA) = Load (L) ÷ Applied Force (*AF*)

If there is a load of 100 lb and a device requiring 10 lb of force to move the load is used, then the MA is 10; 100 lb ÷ 10 lb = 10.

A.   Apparent Mechanical Advantage

To gain any mechanical advantage in moving a load with a block and tackle, a second block attached to the load must be used. Figure 2.6a is a schematic drawing showing a 2-block system with an apparent MA of 2:1. This means that an apparent force equal to half of the load is required to move the load. To determine the apparent mechanical advantage of a block and tackle system, count the number of ropes *supporting* the load. The number of supporting ropes is equal to the theoretical MA. Analyzing the force on the 3 ropes shows that there are 2 ropes supporting the load (S1 and S2), with half the load on each one. To hold the load in position, there is a force of ½ of the load on the *lead line, LL*. A second way to determine the MA is to divide the load by the force required to move the load. If the load equals 1, then L ÷ .5L = 2.

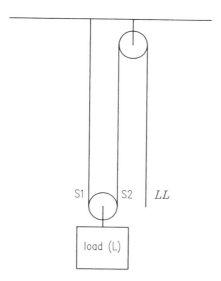

2.6a 2-block system

B. Actual Mechanical Advantage

To raise the load 1′, 2′ of rope must be pulled through the top block (figure 2.6b). When the load is at rest, the tension in the line is equal at all points. When the load is moving, the forces of friction are added to the static force in the line as it passes over a sheave, and the tension in the separate parts of the line is unequal. S1 supports half of the load when moving or static. S2 has the added

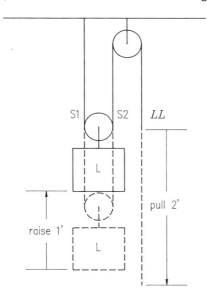

2.6b To raise the load 1′, 2′ of line is pulled through the top block

force required to overcome the friction in the lower block. Assuming that the friction factor is 10%, the tension in S2 is:

.5L + (.5L × 10%) = .55L

The force on *LL* (the lead line pull, *LLP*) includes the friction for the upper block and is:

.55L + (.55L × 10%) = .605L

Therefore, to move the load, we would need a force of .605 of the load plus the force of inertia. Using L ÷ *LLP* = MA, we have 1/.605 = 1.65. The actual mechanical advantage is somewhat less than 1.65 due to inertia.

Adding all of the force on the block and the supporting member when the load is moving, we have:

S1 + S2 + *LLP* = Total load on block and support
.5L + .55L + .605L = 1.655L (or, total load)

Figure 2.7 is a schematic drawing of a 4-line block and tackle with a static mechanical advantage of 4:1. Each of the supporting parts of line, S1 through S4, holds 0.25L when static. The amount of force on the lead line, lead line pull (*LLP*) required to hold the load in the static position is also 0.25L. Every time the rope bends around a sheave, the friction factor for that sheave is added to the pull on the line. Ignoring inertia for the moment, and assuming a 10% friction factor for bearings and rope, the actual dynamic load on each line is:

S1 = .25L
S2 = .25L + (.25L × 10%) = .275L
S3 = .275L + (.275L × 10%) = .3025L
S4 = .3025L + (.3025L × 10%) = .333L
LLP = .333L + (.333L × 10%) = .366L

The total dynamic load on the top block and supporting member, ignoring inertia, is:

S1 + S2 + S3 + S4 + *LLP* = L
.25 + .275 + .303 + .333 + .366 = 1.53L

If we ignore the accumulated friction factor, the apparent dynamic load would be the same as the static load, 1.25L. Taking friction into consideration, the dynamic load is .28L higher than the static load.

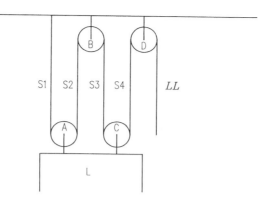

2.7 4-line system

C. Calculating Lead Line Pull

The previous examples illustrate a laborious method of calculating bearing-friction factors and lead line pull. Tables 2.1–2.4 provide information to simplify the calculations. There are 3 numbers in each row in each table. The first is the *number of parts of line (N)*, which refers to the number of supporting lines. The second number, next to the part of line, is the *multiplication factor* (M) used to calculate the load on that part of line. This factor takes into account all of the accumulated sheave friction in the system up to the point of the particular line. The third number is the ratio (R) or *actual mechanical advantage*, on that part of line. This is found by dividing *N* by M (or, *N*/M).

To find the *LLP*, divide the load (L) by the parts of line that give us the theoretical mechanical advantage, and multiply it by M: $LLP = (L \div N) \times M$.

Another way to find *LLP* is to divide the load by the actual mechanical advantage, R. The formula is:

$LLP = L \div R$.

Using the example in figure 2.6b and assigning a value of 500 lb to the load and a friction factor of 10%, and using the value .605 derived for the 2-line system above:

$LLP = 500 \text{ lb} \times .605 = 303 \text{ lb}$

The laborious part is arriving at the number .605. *LLP* can be calculated more quickly using the table to get the value of R:

$LLP = 500 \text{ lb} \div 1.65 = 303 \text{ lb}$

Using R to calculate *LLP* for the 4-line system:

$LLP = 500 \text{ lb} \div 2.74 = 182 \text{ lb}$

Table 2.1   Friction Factors

Friction factor on sheaves
Friction force = 10% of sheave load
Common bearings (hole in the sheave)

Number of Parts of Line (N)	Multiplication Factor (M)	Ratio (R) $R = N/M$ Actual Mechanical Advantage
1	1.10	.91
2	1.21	1.65
3	1.33	2.26
4	1.46	2.74
5	1.61	3.12
6	1.77	3.39
7	1.95	3.59
8	2.14	3.74
9	2.36	3.81
10	2.59	3.86
11	2.85	3.86
12	3.14	3.82
13	3.45	3.77
14	3.80	3.68
15	4.18	3.66

Allowable working loads for different types and sizes of rope are discussed in section 3.03.E. In all of the calculations, the friction caused by the rope rubbing against itself and the force of inertia have been omitted because of the difficulty in calculating them. The actual lead line pull and total load on the system will be greater than the calculated lead line pull. The design factor, or factor of ignorance, allows for this.

D.   Mechanical Advantage of Common Systems

The most common block and tackle systems used for stage rigging have apparent mechanical advantages anywhere from 2:1 to 6:1. There are systems used on cranes with many more parts of line, but they are beyond the scope of this book. Within the range of the systems commonly used for stage work, a number of different

Table 2.2 Friction Factors

Friction factor on sheaves
Friction force = 5% of sheave load
Pressure-lubricated bronze bearings

Number of Parts of Line (N)	Multiplication Factor (M)	Ratio (R) $R = N/M$ Actual Mechanical Advantage
1	1.05	.95
2	1.10	1.80
3	1.16	2.59
4	1.22	3.28
5	1.28	3.90
6	1.34	4.48
7	1.41	4.96
8	1.48	5.40
9	1.55	5.81
10	1.63	6.13

kinds of bearings are used. Each of the bearing types has a finite load limit and a unique coefficient of friction. The load limit is calculated in the overall rating of the block, and you can assume that the WLL has taken the bearing load rating into account.

Many times we do not know what type of bearings the block has, so we must guess at the friction factor. Wooden blocks often have no bearings. The sheaves have a hole punched through them, allowing them to turn on a steel shaft. Lubricant is the only thing that can reduce the friction on this type of block. Judging from the squeaking and groaning heard during operation, there are many unlubricated blocks in use. If you are unsure of the type of bearings in a block, use the 10% friction factor shown in the tables.

Figure 2.8 shows a 5-part system with a mule block added to the lead line to change the direction of the pull. The mule block adds friction to the system and decreases the MA. In this case, the actual mechanical advantage cannot be read directly from the tables. It is calculated by dividing the parts of line supporting the load (N) by the multiplication factor (M) for the number of sheaves the rope passes over.

$R = N \div M$
$R = 5 \div 1.77 = 2.82$

Table 2.3 Friction Factors

Friction factor on sheaves
Friction force = 3% of sheave load
Ball bearings or well-adjusted roller bearings

Number of Parts of Line (*N*)	Multiplication Factor (M)	Ratio (R) R = *N*/M *Actual Mechanical Advantage*
1	1.03	.97
2	1.06	1.89
3	1.09	2.75
4	1.13	3.54
5	1.16	4.31
6	1.19	5.04
7	1.23	5.69
8	1.27	6.30
9	1.30	6.90
10	1.34	7.46

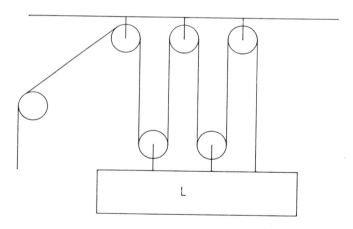

2.8 5-part system with mule block

Without the mule block, R = 5 ÷ 1.61 = 3.11. Therefore *LLP* with the mule block is 500 lb ÷ 2.82 = 177 lb, and without the mule block is 500 lb ÷ 3.11 = 161 lb. Adding a block to a system always decreases mechanical advantage and increases lead line pull.

Figure 2.9 is a 6-part system turned upside down. By reversing the position of the blocks and pulling *up* on the lead line, the lead line becomes a supporting line; the 6-part system becomes a

Table 2.4   Friction Factors

Friction factor on sheaves
Friction force = 1% of sheave load
Excellent precision ball bearings or perfectly adjusted tapered roller bearings

Number of Parts of Line (*N*)	Multiplication Factor (M)	Ratio (R) R = *N*/M *Actual Mechanical Advantage*
1	1.01	.99
2	1.02	1.96
3	1.03	2.91
4	1.04	3.85
5	1.05	4.76
6	1.06	5.66
7	1.07	6.54
8	1.08	7.41
9	1.09	8.26
10	1.10	9.09

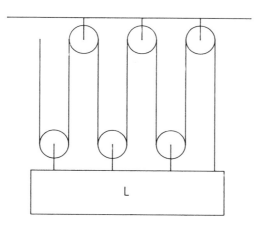

2.9 6-part system upside down

7-part system; and the MA is increased. There are 7 parts of line supporting the load but still only 6 sheaves. To find the mechanical advantage (R) for this system, divide the parts of line supporting the load, *N* (7), by the factor for the number of sheaves (M = 6):

R = 7 ÷ 1.77 = 3.95
LLP = 500 lb ÷ 3.95 = 127 lb

E. Calculating the Total Load on the System

The total load on the system and the supporting member is the load plus the weight of the block and tackle plus the lead line pull. The weight of the load is either calculated or obtained by weighing the object. (If it is large, it can be weighed on a truck scale.)

The weight of the block and tackle is the total weight of the blocks and the line and, depending on the type of equipment, it can be significant. Blocks can range in weight from a few ounces, for an alloy marine block, to over 50 lb, for a 3-sheave 8" block. If it appears that the weight is going to be a significant factor in the total load on the supporting member, weigh the block and tackle on a scale. Once done, label the set for future reference.

LLP can be calculated by using the procedures described above, which is not always possible in the field. Common sense tells us that the maximum load that can be placed on the lead line is equal to the total amount of force available to pull it. In many cases, that would equal the weight of the rigger, or riggers, pulling the line.

A rule of thumb for calculating the total load on the system and supporting member is to add together the weight of the load and the block and tackle system, then double the total. As long as the lines are not twisted, this should provide an adequate design factor for friction and inertia. An exception to this rule is the case of a single-line block, figure 2.4a. A single-line block system exerts a static force of twice the load on the block and supporting member. To determine the total dynamic load on the system and the supporting member and allow for friction and inertia, double the load and add 15% of the load to be raised to the doubled load.

Common block and tackle systems are designed to be used by hand. Attaching the lead line to a capstan winch, forklift, or other mechanical device is not recommended because of the greatly increased applied force on all of the components, which can stress them beyond their capacities.

F. Rope and Sheave Wear

Further analysis of figure 2.7, the 4-sheave system, shows that, to raise the load 1′, 1′ of rope passes around sheave A; 2′ of rope pass over sheave B; 3′ pass over sheave C; and 4′ pass over sheave D. This means that sheave D travels 4 times as fast as sheave A and receives 4 times the wear. The lead line at sheave A has the greatest stress and travels the greatest distance. An example of this kind of stress and fatigue happens to us in everyday life. In lacing up our shoes, we pull on the ends of the laces. The greatest stress and travel of the lace is at the top eyelets, and this is where the lace almost always breaks. Re-reeving the blocks so that the fast sheave becomes the slow sheave and changing the rope end-for-end will equalize the wear on the system and extend the useful life of the rope and the sheaves.

G. Mechanical Advantage of Complex Systems

In section 2.04.D we saw that adding a sheave to a system also added friction to the system. Table 2.1, for 10% friction factors, shows that after 11 parts of line, mechanical advantage actually decreases with the addition of any more parts of line. Using 2 block and tackle systems together, as shown in figures 2.10a and 2.10b, increases the mechanical advantage significantly. The lead line from the 7-part system is attached to the fall block of a 2-part sys-

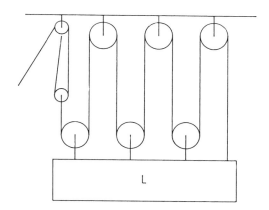

2.10a 2 systems together; 5.92 MA

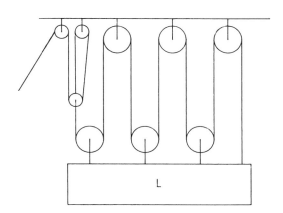

2.10b 2 systems together; 8.11 MA

tem. R is calculated for each system independently: R for the 2-part system is 1.65 and for the 7-part system is 3.59. *When using 2 systems together, the mechanical advantages are multiplied together to calculate the total mechanical advantage acting on the load.* Total actual mechanical advantage:

R = 1.65 × 3.59 = 5.92
LLP = 500 ÷ 5.92 = 84 lb

If 2 additional parts of line had been added to the 7-part system, making it a 9-part system in the same configuration,

R = *N* ÷ M
R = 9 ÷ 2.36 = 3.81
LLP = 500 ÷ 3.81 = 131 lb

R for the 3-part system in figure 2.10b is 2.26. The total mechanical advantage is:

.26 × 3.59 = 8.11
LLP = 500 ÷ 8.11 = 62 lb

While they take more gear and longer to set up, complex systems can significantly increase lifting capacity.

2.05   Lacing and Reeving of Blocks

There are two ways to run the line through a set of blocks. The first, called *lacing* (figure 2.11), runs all of the parts of line in the same direction, starting with a sheave on one side of a block and working toward the other side. Lacing tends to allow the rope to twist a great deal, and in larger systems the block will be inclined

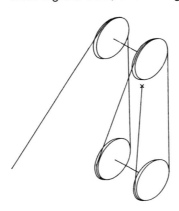

2.11 Laced 4-line system

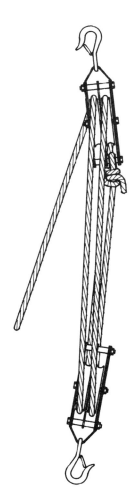

**2.12 Laced
blocks tend to tilt**

to tilt when moving (figure 2.12). When the block tilts, friction is added to the line by rubbing on the cheeks of the block. When the line twists, an enormous amount of friction is added to the system by the line rubbing against itself.

Reeving, the second way to run a line, puts the blocks at right angles to each other. The line passes through the blocks in both directions, and this helps to decrease twisting and reduce friction. When reeving, attach the standing part of the line as close to the center of the block as possible. Also, run the lead line out of a sheave as close to the center as possible; this will reduce the tendency of the block to tilt and allow the line to run without rubbing

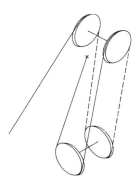

**2.13a Reeving a
4-part system**

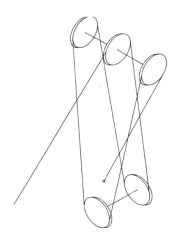

**2.13b Reeving a
5-part system**

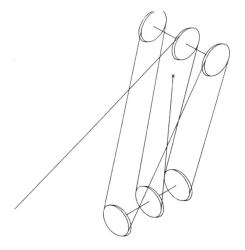

**2.13c Reeving a
6-part system**

on the side plates. Figures 2.13a–2.13c illustrate how to reeve common systems.

2.06 Inspecting a Block and Tackle System

The second K, *knowing that the system is in safe working order*, can only be achieved by periodically inspecting the system. Every time a block and tackle is taken out of storage and set up, the rigger should inspect it. A professional, conscientious rigger inspects every piece of rigging gear before using it. Use the following checklist as a guide.

1. Check the load rating on the blocks. If they are not rated, do not use them for heavy loads. If they are old, use a higher factor of ignorance. Because the parts are worn, they will not be as strong as when they were first made.

2. Look for frayed or worn rope. If it is old Manila or badly worn line of any type, derate the allowable load on the system. See section 3.03.E for additional information on fiber rope.

3. Check to see if the rope is the right size for the sheaves. Too large a rope will rub on the side plates, adding friction and abrading the rope. Too small a rope will not be properly supported by the sheave groove. It may also get jammed between the sheave and the side plate.

4. The hook or attachment device is often the weakest part of a block. Bent or deformed hooks or attachment devices on the blocks may be a sign that the blocks have been overloaded, and the block should be taken out of service. Note the different hook sizes on the blocks in figure 2.14. The single-sheave block is rated for a WLL of 1,000 lb and the double-sheave block is rated for 1,400 lb.

5. Elongated straps or bent side plates are a sign that the block has been overloaded. Remove it from service.

6. Cracked wooden side plates may fall apart under a load. Remove it from service.

7. Turn the sheaves without a load to see if they wobble. Wobbling can be an indication of bad bearings, an oversized hole in the sheave due to wear, or a worn down pin. If the bearings are bad, there is increased friction and increased load on all of the components. A worn pin or enlarged hole in the sheave means a loss of strength of the component. Replace the block.

8. Check all nuts and bolts, rivets, and retaining rings for tightness.

9. Listen to the sheaves. If they squeak, lubricate them sparingly. Do not get lubricant on the line.

2.14 Note the different hook sizes on the blocks

2.07   Using a Block and Tackle System

Before using a block and tackle, make a list of the items that need to be checked and follow it. The user's checklist shown below is a starting point; modify it to fit your needs.

A.   User's Checklist

1. The weight of the load to be lifted
2. The weight of the block and tackle
3. The capacity of the block and tackle to be used
4. The working load limit of the rope
5. The lead line pull
6. The load capacity of the supporting member
7. The total load on the supporting member
8. The location and capacity of the tie-off point for the lead line

B.   Attaching

The standing block is attached to a supporting member. Before climbing up to make the attachment, determine which supporting member the block will be attached to, as well as how it will be attached. Be sure that the supporting member will sustain the load.

You may have to ask a structural engineer to help you. Any sign of deflection in the supporting member is an indication that it may fail.

    1. If a cable basket or choker is to be used, calculate the applied load and size it accordingly. Use a minimum design factor of 5:1 for the wire rope. A minimum design factor of 5:1 is acceptable for wire rope under a static load; a design factor of 8:1 is used for running lines.

    2. If the attachment fitting on the block is a rotating type, mouse it to keep it from rotating (unless for some reason you want it to rotate).

    3. Hook fittings come with and without latches. If there is no latch, mouse the hook to keep it from falling. A good mousing material is solid-core electrical wire. It holds well and can be installed and removed by hand.

    4. Shackles are a positive way to attach the fall block. The shackle should not have a side load on it. The pin may be either up or down.

C.   Operating

    1. Before operating the block and tackle, especially if there are multiple sets in use on a common load, designate one person to be in charge and to give directions to keep the load balanced.

    2. When operating the block and tackle, watch for any deflection on the supporting member. If it starts to deflect, stop immediately, and lower the load to the floor.

    3. Keep the load balanced, so that one rigging point will not have to support more than it should.

    4. If the load spins, tie a tag line to the object and have a rigger stand to the side, holding the line to keep it from spinning.

    5. Keep your concentration.

D.   Storing

There are primarily 2 ways to bundle up block and tackle systems for storage. Once bundled, keep them in a cool, dry place, away from heat sources and contaminants.

    1. Method A. Pull the lead line until the blocks are about 3' apart. Lay them on the floor and coil the line around them. If you are using a right-hand-lay twisted line, coil the line clockwise ("with the sun," as they say in the nautical-rope books). Pull the bundle together, and tie a clove hitch around the bundle in the center. The bundle may be stored by hanging by the top block.

To uncoil, lay the bundle on the floor, clove hitch up. Untie the knot, and carefully take the coiled rope and turn it over. Separate the blocks to the required working distance, feeding the line carefully to avoid tangling.

2. Method B. Separate the blocks to the full extent of the line. Tie the end of the line around the bundle of line just above the fall block. Starting at the standing-block end, coil the bundle and, using *one hand only*, pull the bundle through the loop, making another loop. Using the same hand, continue pulling the bundle through each successive loop until you reach the fall block. Pull the fall block through the last loop. The bundle may now be hung or coiled on a peg for storage.

CAUTION: If you use both hands alternately to pull the line, you create extra twists in the bundle and it is harder to take apart. Also, be very careful that you feed the fall block out *only* through the last loop. It is all too easy to put it through the second-to-last loop. If you do, you will make a series of locking knots that will have to be untied one at a time.

Part 3   Hemp Rigging

3.01   Introduction

Although hemp rigging is the simplest and oldest form of stage rigging, the word *hemp* is actually a misnomer. The term *hemp rigging* generally refers to any fiber rope used for attaching, supporting, or flying stage effects.

3.02   The Hemp Systems

A.   Single-Line System

The simplest system consists of a single rope, a head block, a loft block, a load (something to fly), and a place to tie off the rope (figure 3.1).

Rope. The rope has two ends: the load end, which is usually onstage, and the hauling end, which is usually offstage. Until recently, ½", ⅝", or ¾" No. 1 grade Manila was the rope of preference. Within the last 10 years, synthetic rope has gained acceptance and may replace natural-fiber rope totally.

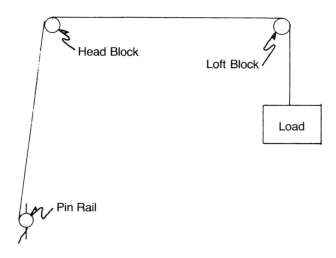

3.1 Single-line hemp set

Head Block

Loft Block

Load

Pin Rail

Head block. The first pulley that the rope passes through, after leaving the rigger's hands, is called the head block. Usually the head block is offstage of the load. (See section 3.04.B.)

Loft block. The pulley that the rope passes through, directly above the load, is the loft block. It is usually onstage. Multiple-line systems have more than one. (See section 3.04.C.)

Spot block. A loft block that is easily movable and can be "spotted," or placed anywhere on the grid, is called a spot block. (See section 3.04.D.)

Pin rail. A rail with vertical pins of wood or metal, used for tying off the hauling end of hemp systems, is known as the pin rail. (See section 3.05.)

B. Multiple-Line System

Two or more lines attached to the same load comprise a multiple-line system. The ropes pass from offstage, through a multisheave head block (see section 3.04), to individual loft or spot blocks, and down to a batten or other object (figure 3.2).

Batten. A pipe or wood rail attached to 2 or more lines of a rigging system is called a *batten*. Loads are attached to the battens. Wood and pipe battens are attached to the hemp lines with a clove hitch and 2 half hitches (figure 3.3).

Line identification. The *lift lines* or *lead lines* on a multiple-line rigging system are identified with reference to their length from the

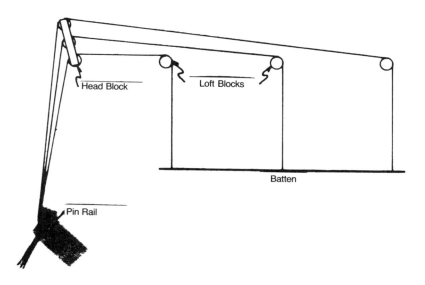

Head Block

Loft Blocks

Batten

Pin Rail

3.2 Multiple-line hemp set

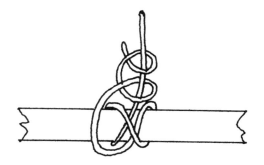

3.3 Tying hemp to a batten

head block. The line nearest the head block is called the short line; the one farther away, the long line (figure 3.4).

Starting from the loft block closest to the head block, typical line designations are as follows:

4-line set: short, short-center, long-center, long
6-line set: short-short, short, short-center, long-center, long, long-long

C. Sandbag and Arbor Attachment as Counterweight

If the load is too heavy for a single stagehand to move, sandbags or arbors for metal weights may be attached to the hauling line. The weight devices are attached by using either a loop of steel

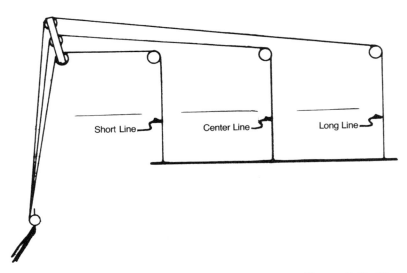

3.4 Hemp-set lift line identification

Short Line

Center Line

Long Line

cable called a *sunday* (figure 3.5) or a trim clamp (figure 3.6). (See section 3.06.)

3.03   The Rope

Rope rigging in the theatre is generally referred to as *hemp rigging*. There are several types of natural-fiber rope that are casually referred to as *hemp*. This practice is confusing, since Manila, not hemp, is the preferred rope for stage rigging. As mentioned earlier, synthetic-fiber rope is gradually being accepted as a viable alternative to natural fiber for rigging use.

A.   Considerations of Rigging Rope

When choosing a fiber rope for rigging, the following characteristics of the rope should be considered.

1. Low Elongation

The rope should not be too elastic. When hauling on the line, the load should rise directly in proportion to the amount of line being pulled, rather than having the line stretch and the load bounce along behind.

2. Flexibility

The rope needs to be flexible enough to tie knots in easily and run over sheaves with a minimum amount of internal friction.

3.5 Sandbag on
a sunday

3. Durability

The rope must be durable enough to withstand the abrasion of running through blocks, being tied off, and generally being used. The rope should also be resistant to atmospheric degradation.

4. Handling Characteristics

The rope should be comfortable to handle. The operator's hands must be able to grasp the line and not slip. The line should tie and coil easily.

5. Strength

The rope must be strong enough to support the load safely and absorb the additional force of friction, inertia, and shock loading for the particular application.

6. Cost and Value

The *cost* of the rope includes the initial purchase price plus the cost of installation. The *value* of the rope is a combination of the ini-

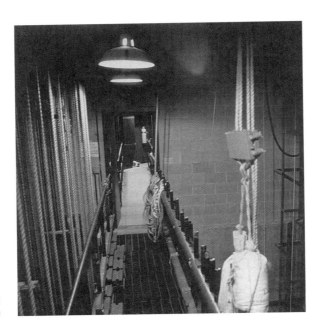

**3.6 Sandbag on
a trim clamp**

tial 2-part cost and the expected life of the rope before it needs to be replaced. If you pay 50% more for a good-quality rope and it lasts 3 times as long as the less-expensive rope, the more-expensive rope is a better value.

B.   Types of Natural-Fiber Rope

The 3 most common types of natural-fiber rope come from living vegetation. All natural-fiber rope has a relatively short strand. The length of the strand is limited by the size of the leaf or stalk from which the fiber is made.

Hemp is a soft fiber made from the inner bark of the main stalk of the cannabis plant. Partly because of the other uses of the leaves of the cannabis, this rope is not readily available in the United States. It is not as strong as Manila.

Sisal is made from the leaf fiber of the agave plant. It is more flexible than Manila but not as strong. It is readily available, less expensive, and easy for the untrained to confuse with Manila. The sisal strands have less cohesion than do Manila strands and, therefore, sisal is not durable enough for rigging. Because it is sometimes used for decorative purposes in the theatre, it is good practice to clearly mark it and store it separately from rigging rope to prevent it from ever being accidentally used for a rigging job.

Manila is a hard fiber made from the leaf of the abaca plant. To add to the confusion, it is sometimes called *Manila hemp*. It possesses the best combination of the desired characteristics of natural-fiber rope for rigging.

Manila is graded by how light it is in color and the cleanliness of the fibers. The lighter the rope, the better the grade. To determine the color of the grade, a light source is focused on the rope, and the amount of reflected light is read on a photometer. The numeric value of the reflected light is called the *Becker value*.

The cleaner and lighter the rope, the longer it will last under acceptable atmospheric conditions. All grades of Manila are manufactured with the same strength rating for each size. The lower the grade, the quicker it will deteriorate and lose its strength. Do not be surprised if your local rope dealer has never heard of the Becker value. It is a term with which, for the most part, only rope experts are familiar.

When purchasing Manila, insist that it be Type M, Class 1, according to federal specification T-R-605B, including Amendment 3, dated 17 April 1973. This specification indicates a minimum Becker value of 36 for Class 1 rope and has the latest minimum strength ratings. (These are the values used in figure 3.9.) Class 2 Manila is not graded by Becker value and generally will not last as long as Class 1. Some Manila is not manufactured to the federal specification at all, and the strength and quality vary widely. If the rope is greater than ½" in diameter and manufactured to the federal specification, it will have a paper tracer in one strand indicating the name of the manufacturer, the year and country of manufacture, and stating that it is Type M, Class 1 Manila (figure 3.7).

Rope can be made in several different ways. Manila rope is almost always twisted. The twisting can be done with either 3 or 4 strands, and the direction of fiber, yarn, and strand twists can vary as well. Different twist directions produce different characteristics in the rope.

The specific method of twisting for stage use is as follows: the fibers are twisted to the right, or clockwise, into yarn. Several pieces of yarn are then twisted to the left, or counterclockwise, and made into strands. Three or 4 strands are twisted to the right, clockwise, to make a rope. This is called a *regular-lay* or *right-lay* rope.

C. Synthetic-Fiber Rope

There are many types of synthetic-fiber rope available. They are braided, cored and mantled, twisted, woven, or any combination of the above. Most of them are not suitable for stage use. Nylon has

3.7 Manila rope with identification tracer

too much stretch and absorbs moisture, making it hard to handle. Polypropylene has a low melting point, low strength, and low abrasion resistance. It floats, but this is not a requirement for stage use.

There are 2 types of polyester rope now manufactured specifically for stage use. They have been in use long enough to have proven their worth and reliability.

1. Parallel-Core Polyester Rope

Parallel-core polyester (left side of figure 3.8) is made of continuous parallel fibers that run the entire length of the rope. The core is wrapped in polyester tape and covered by a braided polyester jacket. Over 95% of the strength of the rope is in the core. Minor abrasion to the jacket does little to reduce the rope's strength. There are no slivers on the rope and it does not degrade in the atmosphere. If it is not overstressed, the life of the rope is almost limitless. The strength-to-size ratio is about 3½ times that of Manila. The polyester is initially more expensive than the Manila, but it lasts much longer and is a much better value in the long run. This rope is a bit stiff for hemp systems, but it makes an excellent hand line for counterweight sets.

2. 3-Strand Twisted Polyester

A 3-strand twisted polyester is also available (right side of figure 3.8) Sizes above ½" diameter are made with spun polyester fibers around a polyolefin core. Sizes with a diameter less than ½" do not have the polyolefin core. This rope has excellent handling characteristics, is easy to tie into knots, and is not susceptible to atmospheric degradation. The breaking strength is a little more than

twice that of Manila. This rope is not as strong as the parallel-core polyester, but it is a bit less expensive. Because it is a 3-strand rope without a jacket, any fiber breakage reduces the strength of the rope. However, unlike Manila, there is no internal organic deterioration. This rope is an excellent substitute for lines in hemp rigging.

D. Tensile Strength or Breaking Strength

Tensile strength is the ultimate strength of the rope before it breaks. (See section 1.06 for a detailed discussion of tensile strength.) The breaking strength of rope should be furnished to you by the rope distributor. Testing is usually conducted and certified by the manufacturer. Figure 3.9 is a comparison chart of tensile strength (in pounds) for hemp, parallel-core polyester, and 3-strand polyester. The actual breaking strength may vary slightly from manufacturer to manufacturer.

E. Strength and Allowable Working Load of Rope

1. Design Factors

The allowable working load is considerably less than the breaking strength. (See section 1.06.H for calculating the allowable load of rope.) Some of the factors affecting the strength of the rope, and therefore the allowable working load, are

a. Strength reduction caused by the knots. EVERY KNOT RE-DUCES THE STRENGTH OF A ROPE, SOME BY AS MUCH AS 50%. (See section 3.03.F.)

Rope Size (in)	Manila	Three-Strand Twist, Polyester	Parallel-Core, Polyester
3/16	406		
1/4	540	1,500	
5/16	900	2,300	
3/8	1,220	3,200	4,600
7/16	1,580	4,100	6,300
1/2	2,380	5,800	8,100
9/16	3,100	6,600	
5/8	3,960	8,230	12,500
3/4	4,860	10,540	16,700
13/16	5,850		
7/8	6,950	15,500	23,000
1	8,100	18,700	32,000
1 1/16	9,450		
1 1/8	10,800		
1 1/4	12,200		

3.9 Rope strength (lb) comparisons. Manila figures courtesy Cordage Institute; polyester figures courtesy New England Rope for Multiline II and Stage-Set X

b. Wear caused by abrasion. Rope rubbing on some part of the grid, an improperly sized sheave, or dirt on the rope will cause the fibers to break and reduce the breaking strength.

c. The potential for shock load. It is easier to break a piece of string with your hands by jerking than by applying steady or constant force. With stage rigging, there is always the chance of a flown piece fouling, then falling, so that a sudden shock load occurs.

d. The length of the rope. The longer the rope, the heavier the load. This is caused by the weight of the rope itself being added to the weight of the load.

e. The type of use. A dead-hung leg in the wing area has less potential for hurting an actor than a working piece, such as a heavy chandelier, over the acting area.

f. Age of Manila rope. Manila, or any natural-fiber rope, is an organic product made from vegetable fiber. It begins to deteriorate in the atmosphere as soon as the plant from which it is made is harvested. Even though there may be no obvious flaws in the rope, it will never be as strong as it was when it was first made. The older the rope, the greater the design factor should be.

2. Factors in Calculating the Allowable Load for Rope

See section 1.06.H for the formula for calculating the allowable load.

a. Breaking strength. Know the rated breaking strength of the size rope being used. Remember that the breaking strength is calculated for new rope and must be derated for older Manila.

b. Weight. Be certain of the weight of the load. Calculate it carefully. If in doubt, weigh the object to be lifted, using truck scales if necessary.

c. Risk. Consider the application and degree of risk to life and property.

d. Strength reduction factors. Consider the strength reduction factors that reduce the ultimate breaking strength of the rope, such as knotting. (See section 3.03.F.)

e. Load increase factors. Consider the load increase factors. These are variable factors that may increase the load above its design limit, such as a curtain absorbing moisture from the atmosphere or distribution of a load on a batten. (See section 3.04.A-2.)

f. Design factor. Allow a minimum 10:1 design factor. The degree of risk to life and property destruction determines the design factor. If there is great risk and the factor of ignorance is great, increase the design factor. THIS DECISION IS YOUR RESPONSIBILITY!

F. Effects of Knotting

Knotting a rope produces sharp bends and shear stresses and thereby reduces the breaking strength. The sharper the bend, the greater the stress concentration, and the greater the damage to the rope. It is interesting to note that under test, the rope will fail next to the knot rather than in the knot itself. A knot should be chosen for its strength, stability, and reduction of injury to the rope. For example, a simple overhand knot, the type that seems to get into the middle of a rope all by itself, can reduce the breaking strength by as much as 75%. If it is left in and stress is applied, a permanent weak spot can develop. See section 6.01.B for the efficiency of common knots.

A 3-strand twisted rope is tested by attaching it to the test machine with eye splices. The breaking strength of a 3-strand rope is actually the breaking strength of that rope with perfect eye splices in it. The eye splices, if properly done are, by definition, 100% efficient. The test splices are made by certified people in a consistent and specified manner. But most of us do not make an eye splice as carefully as they do. Therefore, for field use, the eye splice is derated to 95% efficiency.

G. Care of Rope

Rope is a tool made from organic or synthetic fibers. For it to perform properly within its design parameters, you must correctly care for it.

1. Balance

A rope made by twisting has a certain amount of twist built into it. If the rope has too much twist, it will kink or get a *hockle* in it. If it has too little twist, it loses strength. When the twist is just right, the rope is *in balance*. Try to avoid twisting stranded rope while working with it. If it becomes kinked from too much twist, it must be untwisted to restore proper balance. In stagehands' jargon, this is known as "taking the assholes out of the rope." This can be done either by actually twisting the rope in the direction opposite to the final strand twist or, preferably, by hanging it vertically. If the end is allowed to hang free from the grid or fly floor, the excess twist will usually come out by itself. If the kink is not removed and a load is placed on the line or it is pulled through a confined space, such as a head block or loft block, permanent damage to the rope will occur. If there is too little twist in the rope, with strands hanging loose from each other, the rope has been damaged and should not be used for rigging.

2. Uncoiling Rope

New rope in a full coil is stiff and has a tendency to stay curled. The proper way to uncoil it is to lay the coil down on its side, so the inside end is down near the floor. Begin uncoiling the rope from the inside end, turning it in your hand to remove the excess twist. This method will keep the rope from tangling and kinking.

3. Coiling Rope

When finished working with a rope, coil it properly. *Never coil a twisted rope over your hand and elbow*, as this will put excess twist in the rope and cause kinking. Right-laid rope should be coiled clockwise, or "with the sun." Care should be taken to remove all excess twist. Do this by turning the rope as it is being coiled.

If the rope is properly coiled and in balance, no twisting or kinking of individual coils should occur. Rope can be coiled over an open hand, on a pin of the pin rail, or if too long and heavy, flat on the floor. When coiling a rope on the floor, be sure that the top coils do not get larger and fall around the bottom coils. This will cause kinking and tangles the next time you use the rope. If coiling a long length of rope that is to be used again immediately, let it pile up in figure-8 coils. *Do not try to pick up the rope when it is coiled in figure 8s.*

4. Storing Rope

On a fly floor, rope should be dressed or properly coiled and hung on a belaying pin. *Do not leave it lying around on the floor.* It will pick up dirt and is dangerous for the stagehand to walk on. (See section 3.03.G-5.) Sometimes rope is stored near or on the grid, as spot lines must be rigged from there. Provide some method of hanging the rope, preferably on wooden pegs so that air can circulate freely through it. Natural-fiber rope absorbs moisture from the air. If it is hung on a metal peg or on a metal surface, the metal can oxidize and hasten the deterioration of the rope.

5. Keeping Rope Clean

Grit and dirt work into the fibers of the rope and break them through abrasion. Dust absorbs the dressing put on the rope during manufacture and dries it out, thus shortening life. When a rope gets dirty, wash it in clear water. Pass it through a tub of water, and swish it around until the dirt comes out, or hose it off. A mild dishwashing detergent can be used but should be thoroughly rinsed out.

6. Drying Rope Properly after Wetting

Because Manila is an organic substance, it will rot or mildew if stored wet. Hang it loosely where dry air can circulate, and dry it thoroughly. Inspect the rope for dryness by untwisting it a bit and touching and smelling the fibers. Wet Manila has a distinctive odor. Polyester will not rot, but it still needs to be thoroughly dried after wetting.

7. Protecting Rope from Chemicals

Acidic and alkaline substances will harm Manila fibers. Grease and oil destroy the fiber friction that holds rope together. Paint solvent dries out rope. Polyester rope is not as affected by harsh chemicals. Nevertheless, keep all rope away from chemicals.

8. Avoiding Rope Overload

Once a rope is stressed beyond its elastic limit, it loses its original strength. Use the right rope size for the job at hand. If it is overstressed, take it out of service and destroy it. NOTE: If you throw away a rope, cut it up. If someone uses your cast-off rope for load-bearing or lifeline applications and it fails, you could be liable. Always cut up old rope before throwing it away.

9. Avoiding Sharp Bends and Small Sheaves

A rope tied around a sharp corner of a heavy load can be strained at that point, which will permanently weaken the rope. Pad all sharp corners. When a rope passes around a sheave, it bends as it moves. Be sure that the pulley has a large enough diameter so that the rope will not be severely strained. (See section 4.06.B.) Maintain a minimum ratio of sheave diameter to rope diameter (D/d ratio) of 8:1.

10. Avoiding Abrasion

Do not drag rope over rough surfaces. Doing so will cause unnecessary wear. Sheaves or pulleys must be grooved for the size rope being used. If the groove is too small, the friction on the rope will cause it to wear and weaken. Be sure that blocks are aligned so that the rope does not rub on side plates.

11. Avoiding Shock Load

Jerking a rope or suddenly dropping a load (such as when a fouled piece of rigging falls free) can easily break a rope. One of the reasons that the safe working load is much less than the breaking strength of a rope is to allow for this possibility. The greater the shock load, the easier it is to break the rope. If a rope is subjected to a severe shock load, it may be stressed beyond its elastic limit. If a rope has been shock loaded, take it out of service.

12. Adjusting Rope for Humidity

Humidity affects Manila rope. As the humidity increases, the fibers absorb the moisture from the air and swell. The rope gets thicker and shorter. As the humidity drops, the rope dries out; the fibers shrink in diameter, and the rope gets longer. In environments where there is significant change in humidity, such as in theatres with intermittent air-conditioning or outdoors, multiple-line hemp sets must be trimmed before every performance. Because the lines are different lengths on multiple-line sets, they will not shrink or expand evenly. A hanging drop, level at low humidity, will get high on the long side as the humidity increases. In this case, the load is free to move, and no damage will be done to the rope.

In some instances, where the load cannot move, such as a guy rope, permanent damage to the rope may occur owing to shrinkage caused by dampness. The rope can get stretched past its elastic limit and lose some of its tensile strength. In such cases, it is important to remember to slack off the tension on the rope as it contracts. Polyester rope is not affected by humidity and therefore needs no adjustment.

13. Inspect Rope Periodically

Using the rope until it breaks is irresponsible. As you use it, *be aware of it; look at it; feel it!* If something does not feel or look right, replace it, rather than take a chance. *Visually inspect all rigging rope over its complete length on a regular basis.* This is best accomplished by unrigging it and inspecting the entire length by hand and eye. For multiline hemp sets, have someone on the grid at the head block inspect the line as the set is raised and lowered. (See section 3.03.E.)

14. Rotating Rope Position

Periodically change around the ropes. Reverse the ends and change the jobs they do. This will avoid causing weak spots, spread the wear throughout rope, and increase the life of the rope.

THINK: All of the above recommendations for taking care of rope are common sense! Take the time to care for the rope. Replacing rope is expensive. Replacing a life is impossible.

H.   Indications of Wear

When inspecting any kind of rope, look for the following:

Indentations. Indentations are caused by a kink being pulled through a block or excess strain.

Wear. A rough or worn spot, wear, is caused by abrasion and broken fibers and yarns. Any broken fiber in a 3-strand rope or in the core of a parallel-strand rope means a reduction in strength. Open up the strands on a twisted rope. Signs of internal wear are a powdery residue or broken strands inside.

Variation in color. Color variations are indications of chemical contamination. Take the rope out of service.

Variation in diameter. Reduction in diameter is an indication of overload or excessive wear on the rope.

Broken internal strands. Open up twisted rope and look for broken internal strands. The internal strands can be the first to break when a rope has been overstressed.

High strand. If one strand is either higher or lower in a twisted rope, the load is not being evenly distributed on all of the strands and the rope cannot sustain its rated load (figure 3.10).

Dryness. Untwist a strand and break a few fibers between your fingers. Overly dry rope will break easily.

Wetness. A wet rope loses a great deal of its strength. *If it is wet, do not use it.* Dry it well before using.

Rot. Untwist the rope in several places. Look on the inside

3.10 3-strand-twist Manila with high strand

80

where the strands touch each other for signs of mildew and rot, which is indicated by odor and by darker-colored fibers.

Acid contamination. A dark spot or a dark area on the rope can be an indication of acid or chemical contamination. Many of the chemicals that are used for painting, dying, and cleaning backstage contain enough acid to be harmful to rope.

All of the preceding conditions reduce the strength of the rope. Do not use a rope with any of the above conditions for rigging. Take it out of service and destroy it.

I. Testing a Rope

1. Manila Rope

If you are not sure of the strength of a rope, do not guess. Manila rope loses strength every day. It is organic and gradually deteriorates even while it is just sitting there. If a nearby college or university engineering school has testing equipment, ask them to run a destructive test on a sample for you. If there is no free testing facility available, contact a professional testing laboratory. The only way to determine the strength of Manila rope is to perform a destructive test on it. If that is not possible, rig the rope as it is to be used and then load it to a *minimum* of 5 times the anticipated working load. The rope should perform within its elastic limit and should return to its original length after the load is removed with no signs of overstress. If the rope stretches to the point of deformation, or if there are other signs of overstress, do not use it. While this procedure is time-consuming, it is better than having the rope break while in use. Remember, the greater the risk in a given situation, the greater the design factor needed. Do not keep old, unsafe rope around. Cut it up and dispose of it so that it does not get used by a person who does not know that it is weak.

2. Synthetic Rope

Unless you purchased a synthetic rope and are sure of its type, strength, and history of use, do not assume the strength. Many types of synthetic rope look similar. The rope could have been shock loaded or misused without your knowledge. Test it, or get new rope that you are sure of.

J. Bo'sun's Chair

A rope that has been used for flying scenery or for lifting any material should never be used for rigging a bo'sun's chair or for any type of life- or fall-protection line. To do so is against the law, as well as being highly dangerous. There are special requirements for rope used to lift or protect people. Check the current OSHA regulations.

K. Selecting the Right Rope for the Job

1. For general hemp rigging, choose Type M, Class 1 Manila, or polyester of the appropriate size.

2. Choose rope of the proper diameter to hold the expected load, making certain that it is compatible with the blocks available for the job. Common sizes of blocks are ½" and ⅝". Half-inch rope will work quite nicely in ⅝" sheaves, but ⅝" rope will be chewed to shreds by ½" sheaves.

3. Request test reports from your supplier.

4. Whip ends to keep them from unraveling. (See section 6.01.A-1.)

5. Uncoil it properly.

6. Post the safe working loads backstage in a prominent place, so that all technicians will have the information available when and where they need it—working backstage with the rope.

7. Mark various lengths of rope by color-coding the whipped ends or in some other way. It is difficult to distinguish between a 125′ rope and a 150′ rope when they are coiled up on a dark grid. Post a sign explaining the marking system on the grid, in the fly gallery, and on floor level.

8. Inspect all rope periodically and replace it if you have *any* doubts about its condition.

3.04   Blocks

Hemp-rigging *blocks* are pulleys that are used to change the direction of the force that moves a load. A block consists of the following parts (figure 3.11): (1) sheave, (2) bearings, (3) shaft or axle, (4) side plates, (5) retainers, (6) base angle, (7) keeper pin.

1. Sheaves. The *sheave* is a grooved wheel. The groove should be sized to support at least ⅓ of the rope's circumference. The edges of the groove should be flared enough to allow the rope to enter and exit the groove without abrasion (figure 3.12). As a rec-

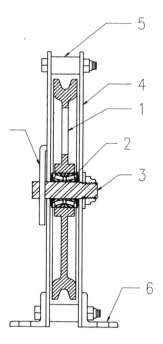

3.11 Block

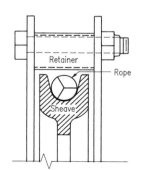

Retainer

Rope

Sheave

3.12 Rope sheave

ommended guideline, the minimum tread diameter of the sheave should be 8 times the rope's diameter (figure 3.13).

2. Bearings. The *bearings* reduce the friction between the sheave and the shaft. Typically, either some type of ball bearings or tapered roller bearings are used in hemp-rigging blocks. See sections 2.03 and 2.04 for detailed information on bearings and friction factors. Of the many types of bearings, some require periodic lubrication, and some are permanently lubricated and sealed. The

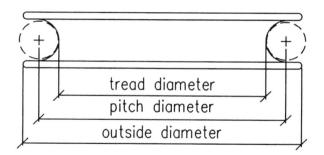

tread diameter

pitch diameter

outside diameter

sealed bearings may eventually dry and have to be replaced. If the sheave does not turn easily or if it squeaks, there is a bearing problem that should be analyzed and corrected.

3. Shaft. The *shaft* should be large enough to support the required load. It must be attached to the side plates to prevent the shaft from rotating. All rotational action should be limited to the sheave.

4. Side plates. The *side plates*, made of steel, support the shaft. The retainers and other spacers keep the side plates evenly separated.

5. Retainer. The *retainer*, usually a length of pipe or tubing held in place by a bolt, prevents the rope from jumping out of the sheave groove. The diameter of the retainer is usually larger than the bolt to allow the position of the retainer to be adjusted relative to the sheave. Retainers should not be placed too close to the sheave or they will rub on the rope or sheave. They can usually be adjusted slightly by loosening the bolt and moving it closer or farther away from the sheave (figure 3.14).

6. Mounting device. The *mounting device* holds the block to the support steel. A block will have a tendency to move in the direction of the resultant force. (See section 1.04.A.) The mounting device should provide metal-to-metal contact in the direction opposite the applied force. This is especially important in preventing horizontal

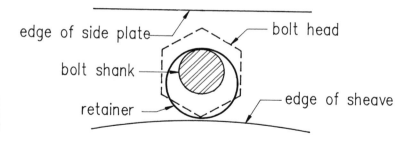

edge of side plate

bolt head

bolt shank

**3.14 Section
through a
retainer and bolt**

retainer

edge of sheave

84

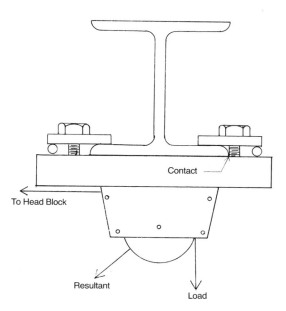

3.15 Underhung block

Contact

To Head Block

Resultant

Load

movement (figure 3.15). *At a minimum, grade 5 bolts should be used for all block mounting.*

A. Loads

To calculate the load, it is necessary to understand the forces that are applied to the block.

1. Applied and Resultant Forces

Two forces are applied to a block at any given time: the force of the load and the force that holds or moves the load. These combined forces produce a resultant force (figure 3.16). See section 1.04 for a detailed discussion about the summation of forces.

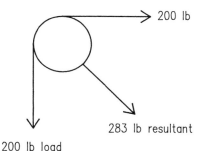

3.16 Applied and resultant force diagram, 90°

200 lb

283 lb resultant

200 lb load

2. Batten Loading

A *batten* is a continuous beam (see section 1.03.G), and an evenly distributed load on the batten produces resultants of different magnitudes on the lift lines. The resultants can be calculated using the 3-moment theorem—a very laborious process and beyond the scope of this book. Figure 3.17 shows the percentage of the total load that is applied to each loft block and lift line on a batten. The percentages are based on the assumptions that the lift lines are evenly spaced, the load is evenly distributed, and the end lines are at the ends of the battens. When trimming a line set, it is possible to feel the difference in weight from line to line.

On a 3-line set (second row from the top in figure 3.17), the end lines each support 18.75% of the total weight, and the center line supports 62.5% of the total weight. Moving the end lines in toward the center increases the load on the end lines and decreases the load on the center point. However, we do not always hang evenly distributed loads. If the batten extends too far out past the end-line and a leg is hung on the end, the batten will sag, and the curtain will not hang straight.

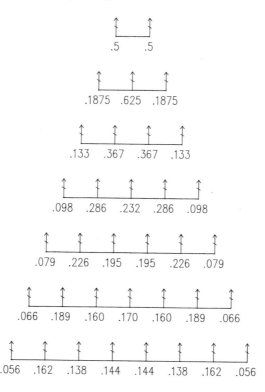

3.17 Reactions of evenly distributed load on lift lines and loft blocks (numbers are percentages of total load on batten). Courtesy Peter Albrecht Corporation

B. Head Blocks

Two types of head blocks are most commonly used for hemp sets. One type has all of the sheaves mounted on a single shaft (figure 3.18). The resultant force on this type of block is similar to that on loft blocks.

The other type stacks the sheaves on separate shafts (figure 3.19). The resultant force usually runs in a direction fairly close to

3.18 Single-shaft head block

3.19 Stacked head block

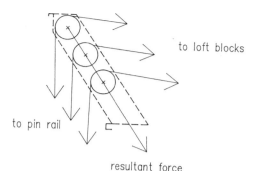

3.20 Resultant force on stacked head block

3.21 Grid-mounted loft block

the center line of the long dimension of the side plates. This places the majority of the load on the bottom block support (figure 3.20).

C. Loft Blocks

Loft blocks can be either mounted on the grid (figure 3.21) or underhung on support steel over the grid (figure 3.22). (See section 3.04.F.)

D. Spot Blocks

Loft blocks that are designed to be easily movable are called *spot blocks*. Extreme care must be taken to see that spot blocks are se-

3.22 Underhung loft blocks with idler pulleys. Courtesy Peter Albrecht Corporation

curely mounted. The V-shaped piece of steel on the underside of the block in figure 3.23 is designed to fit tightly against the grid steel to prevent horizontal slippage.

The V shape allows the block to be mounted at an angle to the grid steel in order to maintain a proper fleet angle with the head block. (See section 3.08.C.)

E. Mule Blocks

Mule blocks change the direction of lift lines in the horizontal plane.

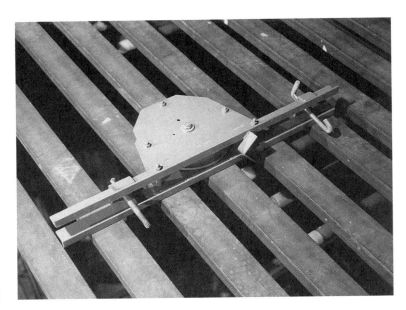

3.23 Spot block

This type of block is used when it is not possible to run the lift line straight from the head block to the loft block (figure 3.24).

F. Idler Pulleys

Nonload-bearing blocks are called *idler pulleys*. Their function is to keep the lift lines from sagging on long runs from head blocks to loft blocks (see figure 3.22). These are usually found on systems where the loft blocks are underhung from the roof steel. Since an idler pulley does not bear any of the lifting load, it can be of a much lighter construction than a loft or head block.

G. Sag Bars

Sag bars (figure 3.25) are used on grid-mounted systems to keep the running lines from fouling on the blocks that they have to pass. They are usually made from hardwood. Attaching a strip of ultra-high-molecular-weight plastic (UHMW) to the top of the wood greatly increases the life of the bars. The sag bars also tend to eliminate much of the cable noise and provide for quieter operation of the system.

3.24 Mule blocks. Courtesy Peter Albrecht Corporation

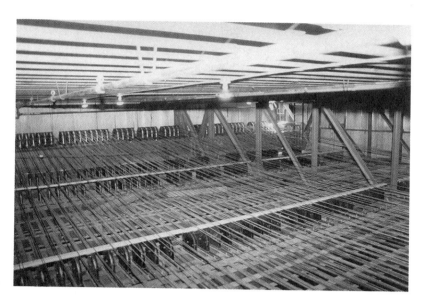

3.25 Sag bars on top of grid-mounted loft blocks

H.   Snatch Blocks

Snatch blocks open so that a lift line can be placed on the sheave without being threaded through from the end. Snatch blocks are handy for muling or idler purposes, after the load has been attached to a lift line (figure 3.26).

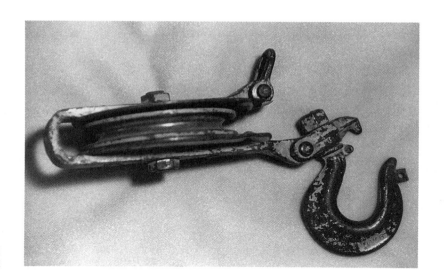

3.26 Snatch block

3.27 Rescue block

For temporary rigging, a rescue block can be used to divert or align a line. These are lightweight blocks that open easily and are found in mountain-climbing stores. The sheaves are made of lightweight material and should *not* be used for wire rope (figure 3.27).

3.05　Pin Rail

The *pin rail* is used to tie off, or *belay,* the hauling end of a hemp system. The rail is a horizontal wooden beam or a large pipe, pierced with vertical pins. The pins are made either of hardwood or of pipe. They can be either fixed to the rail or removable.

A. Fixed Pin Rail

As the name *fixed pin rail* implies, the pins are permanently attached and cannot be removed. This type of rail is safer than the loose pin rail for cinching a load, in that the pins cannot work themselves out as the rope passes around the pin. Another advantage is that the pins cannot be lost.

B. Loose Pin Rail

On a loose pin rail, the pins are removable. It is possible to release the tie-off by pulling the pin out, which should never be done if there is a load on the line. If there is only one wrap around the pin, the pin spins as the load is eased in. Because of that spin, there is little friction on the rope. A second wrap around the top of the pin in the opposite direction eliminates the spin, increases the friction, and gives greater control over the load. The pins can be removed to clear space for extra large coils of rope hanging on the rail.

C. Single Pin Rail

A single pin rail is, as the name implies, one rail. High and low trim are tied off on adjacent pins.

D. Double Pin Rail

The double pin rail (figure 3.28) consists of two rails. The top rail is usually set further onstage than the lower rail. Tie off high trim on one rail and low trim on the other.

E. Pins

The pins can be made of hardwood or steel. Hardwood pins are easier on the rope. They do not promote rust in damp climates, but because they are usually loose, they spin when letting in a load. If used on a steel pin rail, hardwood pins become indented from spinning under side load and lose strength due to the broken wood fiber at the point of indentation (figure 3.29). Examine the pins for broken wood fibers, especially at the lower point of contact with the pin rail. If they are indented, take them out of service.

Steel pins can either be solid or made from pipe. Loose steel

3.28 Double pin rail

3.29 Belaying pins with indentations at lower contact points

pins will also spin but are not susceptible to the wearing that wood pins are vulnerable to. Pins made from pipe should have the ends plugged to prevent riggers from inadvertently catching their fingers in the hole. More than one rigger has missed a cue due to getting a finger stuck (figure 3.30).

3.30 Finger in pin (Don't do this!)

F. Tying Off

There is a specific procedure for tying off a hemp line or set.

1. Take a single wrap around the underside of the pin (figure 3.31). The friction of the rope on the pin immediately gives the operator some control of the load. It is always best to raise the load a little too high, make the wrap, and then ease it into trim position. If the load is very heavy or on a loose pin rail, 2 or 3 wraps may be necessary to control the load.

2. Cross the rope on the face of the rail and take a wrap around the top of the pin (figure 3.32).

3. Make another wrap around the underside of the pin, in the same direction as the first wrap.

4. Form a loop by twisting the rope. The free end goes under the standing part (figure 3.33).

5. Put the loop over the top of the pin (figure 3.34).

6. Pull it tight (figure 3.35).

Never tie off on the first wrap. By tying off after least 4 wraps, you are able to maintain control of the load after untying the line because the other 3 wraps are still around the pin.

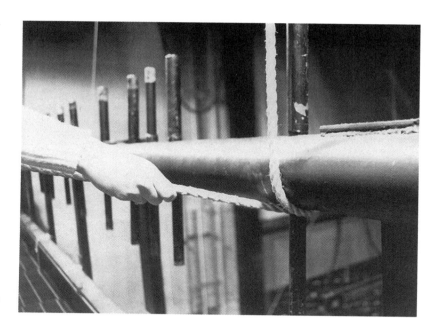

**3.31 Tying off,
step 1**

**3.32 Tying off,
step 2**

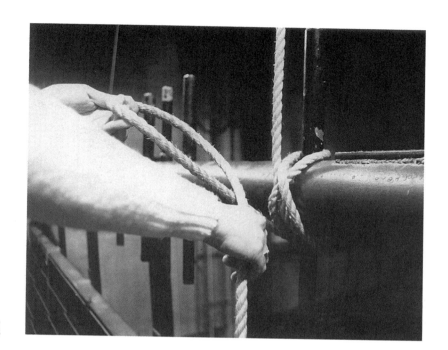

3.33 Tying off,
step 3

3.34 Tying off,
step 4

3.35 Tying off,
step 5

3.06   Sandbags and Arbors

Sandbags are usually used as counterweight for hemp rigging.
They are made of heavy canvas that has been reinforced with rope
or nylon straps. The rope or strap has a snap hook affixed to it for
easy attachment to the lift lines. Sandbags commonly range in size
from 10 lb to 150 lb. Add or remove sand from the bags as
needed, to match the weight of the load. There should be a con-
tainer on the fly floor to hold extra sand.

Metal weights on a single rod arbor are sometimes used instead
of sandbags. This hardware is only manufactured under special order and is not readily available. The arbor is attached to the lift
lines in the same way that sandbags are attached. The weight on
the arbor can be adjusted by adding or subtracting weights from
the arbor rod. The rods can be tied to the lift line at the top and bottom to keep the weight from swinging (figures 3.36 and 3.37).

A.   Attaching Sandbags and Arbors with a Sunday

One method of attaching weight devices to the lift line is to use a
loop of steel cable, called a *sunday*. A piece of ⅛" steel cable, 3' to

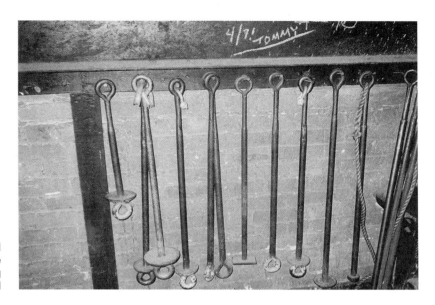

3.36 Metal rod arbors in storage position along rail wall

4′ long, is formed into an endless loop, either by using Nicopress sleeves (see section 6.02.C-2) or by tying a water knot (also known as a *sunday knot*) in it (figure 3.38). Many theatres have started using sundays made from 5- to 6-mm Kevlar or Spectra rope. Spectra and Kevlar are stronger than steel cable. The knots are easier to tie; the rope is more flexible than cable; and the rope is easier on the hand line. Spectra and Kevlar rope can be purchased at sporting goods stores that carry mountain-climbing gear.

The sunday is attached to the lift line by wrapping the loop around the lift line and passing one end of the loop through the other (figure 3.39).

The weight device is then hung on the remaining loop (see figure 3.5).

B. Attaching Sandbags and Arbors with a Trim Clamp

Another method of attaching sandbags and arbors to the lift lines is to use a trim clamp. The clamp is bolted over the ropes with the steel loop facing down. Sometimes it helps to squeeze the trim clamp together with a C-clamp when putting it on. There are spring-loaded jaws inside the trim clamp that must be compressed in order to tighten the nuts (figure 3.40). The sandbags are then hung on the loop (see figure 3.6).

The advantage of using a trim clamp is that the load is easier to retrim after the trim clamp and sandbags are attached than with a

3.37 Metal rod arbors on hemp lines

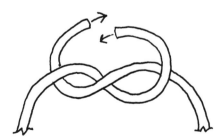

3.38 Sunday knot

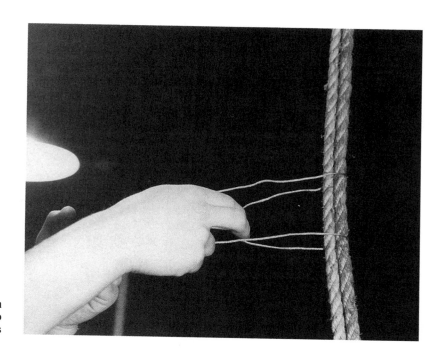

3.39 Attaching a sunday to hemp lines

3.40 Trim clamp

sunday. This is done by pulling the longest lines through the clamp, thus raising the low points. If there is an unevenly distributed load, it may be necessary for someone on the stage floor to hold down the flown piece at the high points while the low points are raised. Rather than hold the piece directly, the rigger can tie a tag line to the batten at these points. (See section 6.05.C.)

3.07   Jack Line

A *jack line* is a separate line that runs over a block on the grid. One end is tied to the sunday or trim clamp on the lift lines, and the other end is tied to a separate pin. In some theatres, the jack line system is along the side wall of the stage, on the opposite side of the fly gallery from the pin rail. The jack line is used to let the flown piece in when it is bag-heavy. By pulling up on the jack line, the flown piece is lowered (figure 3.41).

3.08   Spot Line Rigging

Hemp sets can be positioned, or *spotted*, for special production needs. Either single- or multiple-line sets can be used to provide

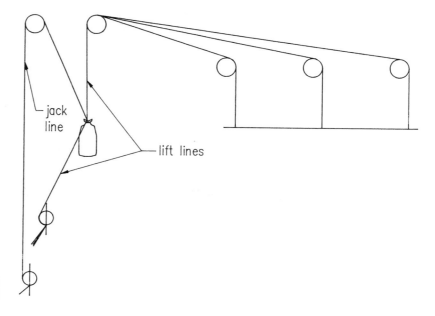

3.41 Jack line schematic

flying capability in positions and patterns to supplement permanently installed batten sets.

A. Positioning Loft Block

Installing a spot line set begins with positioning the loft block. The point where the lift line must drop is usually determined on the stage floor. A target that is easily visible from the grid is placed on the floor. Using a plumb bob, a weight on the lift line, or the "spit method," position the block on the grid directly above the target (or as close as possible). The loft block is then lined up with the drop point over the target, and the sheave is aligned with the head block position. The block is then secured to the grid.

NOTE: It is most important that the block be firmly mounted, so that there is no chance of the block slipping. (See section 3.04.D.)

B. Positioning Head Blocks

Once the loft blocks are firmly attached, the head blocks are aligned with the loft blocks and secured in place. It is important that the rope travel in a straight line from the head block's sheave to the spot block's sheave to avoid abrasion to the rope. When using the type of head block with the sheaves mounted side by side, it is sometimes necessary to angle the spot blocks slightly to align them properly.

C. Fleet Angle

The *fleet angle* (*FA*) is the angle the line makes when two blocks are offset from each other relative to a straight line from the center point of one sheave (figure 3.42). For stage rigging, the maximum acceptable fleet angle is 1.5° (figure 3.43). The formula for calculating the fleet angle is:

$\tan FA = a \div b$
a = offset distance
b = distance between the pins of the sheaves

You must use the same units for both dimensions (inches, feet, centimeters, etc.).

Using a calculator with trig. functions, find the tangent according to the formula, push the inverse tan keys, and read the degrees. If the angle is equal to or less than 1.5°, the fleet angle is acceptable. If it is greater than 1.5°, there is a possibility of abrasion on

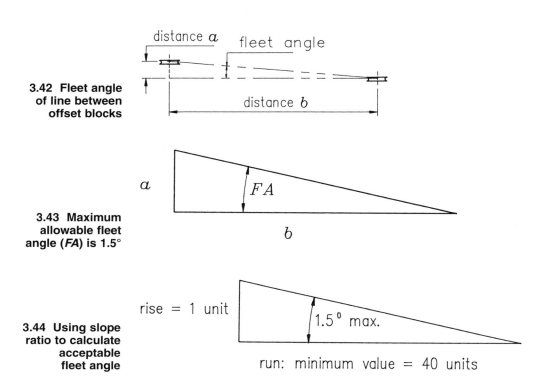

3.42 Fleet angle of line between offset blocks

distance a fleet angle

distance b

3.43 Maximum allowable fleet angle (*FA*) is 1.5°

a FA

b

3.44 Using slope ratio to calculate acceptable fleet angle

rise = 1 unit

$1.5°$ max.

run: minimum value = 40 units

the line and excessive side load on the bearings. Mule blocks may be required to correct the problem.

A quick method of approximating the fleet angle is to look at it in terms of slope. The rise is the offset, and the run is the distance between the pins of the blocks. Anything less than 1 ÷ 40, such as 1 ÷ 50, is acceptable. Anything greater, such as 1 ÷ 30, and the angle is too great (figure 3.44).

D. Aligning Blocks

When using a head block with side-by-side sheaves, align the short loft block with one of the inside sheaves. Use the adjacent inside sheave for the short center and the outside sheaves for the long center and long lines. The worst fleet angle case is with the short line. Make that run as close to a straight line as possible. You need to calculate the fleet angle for all of the lift lines, and adjust the position of the head block or provide muling as required (figure 3.45).

Starting with an outside sheave for the short line causes a

3.45 Least fleet angle for all blocks

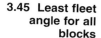 

3.46 Greatest fleet angle for long center line

greater offset for the long center line, and it may exceed a 1.5° fleet angle (figure 3.46).

E. Running Rope

Once the blocks are positioned, the rope is fed through the blocks from the grid. Attach a weight, or tie off the rope as soon as it is fed through the blocks, to keep it from running away. Storing the rope somewhere near the grid eliminates the necessity of hauling the rope to the grid every time a spot line must be run.

F. Attaching Weight to Rope

The onstage end of the rope should be either attached immediately to the load or weighted. Weighting can be done with a small sandbag or by running the end of the line through a short section of pipe and tying a figure-8 knot in the end of the line (figures 3.47 and 3.48).

3.09   Operation of Hemp Rigging

The safe operation of hemp rigging requires a thorough knowledge of how the rigging system works. This knowledge includes knowing the function of each of the components and knowing how the components work together to make an integrated system. Hemp rigging requires of riggers more physical strength to operate than do other types of rigging. At times, the operator will need to move unbalanced loads solely by brute strength. Because almost all lift line connections are knots, the operator must also have a thorough knowledge of knot tying. Both strength and knowledge must be properly applied. Concentration and attention to detail are essential to the safe operation of hemp rigging. In brief:

1. Know the rigging system you are working with.
2. Know that it is in safe working order.

3.47 Rope weighted with sandbag

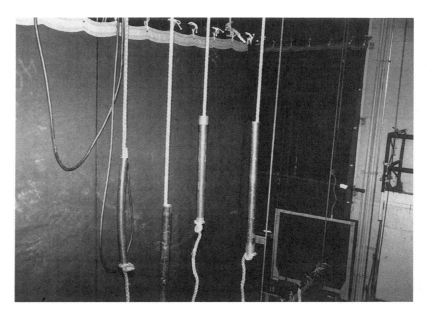

3.48 Rope weighted with pipe

3. Know how to use it.
4. Keep your concentration.

A. Safety Inspecting All Components

The components of a rigging system should be thoroughly inspected on a periodic basis. The resident technician, house carpenter, or technical director is responsible for maintaining the equipment. It is this person's job to see that the rigging system is in perfect working order. It is the management's responsibility to provide the time for maintenance. The system should be inspected, component by component, *at least* once a year. If the resident technician does not have sufficient expertise to conduct an inspection, it will be necessary to hire an outside expert to do it. Have a competent person not familiar with the equipment periodically perform the inspection: an outside set of eyes can often spot things that are missed by the people who have grown accustomed to the system. (See section 3.11.)

In a strange theatre, if there is a high degree of risk, always inspect the rigging before attaching loads. Never assume that, just because it is there, the rigging is in good condition.

Knowing a rigging system goes beyond a knowledge of the parts and their locations. Every rigging system is unique and has its own feel, sound, and smell. Becoming aware of these sensory perceptions is essential, so that every time the system is used, there will be instant awareness if something is out of the ordinary. A sheave with dry bearings or a rope being rubbed makes a distinct sound. It feels different. A piece of hemp with dry rot or hemp that has been charred by a lighting instrument has a distinct smell. Knowing how the system should be when it is in perfect operating condition is a prerequisite to spotting problems.

Keep the floor, grid, and fly gallery clean. Any sign of foreign substances, such as metal filings or rope fibers, is a sign that something is wearing. Keeping the work area clean makes it easier to see these signs of wear.

B. Untying a Line Set

Before untying the line on a hemp set, grasp the rope above the pin and pull it. Get a feel for the load that is on the line before you untie it. Make this a habit. If the rope is quite taut, it is a signal to be extremely cautious when untying the line. The load is probably very heavy. Keep several wraps around the pin, so that you can safely control the line set. If the load is heavier than you are and you untie it completely, it will be impossible to hold. If you do not let go immediately, it will haul you up to the head block. Riggers have been seriously injured and killed by having a line set run away with them.

C.   Attaching Loads

Most of the time, loads are attached at stage-floor level. The rail operator should lower the load end of the rope to the stage floor. Before moving any piece of rigging during a load-in or strike, always alert the people onstage and on the grid by yelling a clear warning to the stage. If the rail operator cannot see the load, a spotter should be used. The spotter watches the load and communicates directly with the rail operator. Be sure that the components are within an adequate design factor for the degree of risk. If the loads are very heavy, it may be necessary to join or marry two or more line sets. (For specific information on attaching techniques, see part 6.)

Once the load is attached, it is pulled up to the low-trim position. Several people may be required to raise the load, but one competent person must be assigned to the task of tying off the rope. At this point, multiple-line sets are *trimmed*, which means that the individual lines are pulled level to the stage floor or relevant low-trim datum point. The rope is then tied off.

With the low trim tied off, the flown piece is then raised to its high-trim position and tied off again. At this point, sandbags or (an arbor) are attached, and the load is balanced. (Enough weight should be added to the offstage end to ensure ease of operation. However, if there is no jack line, the line set must be slightly load-heavy in order to operate.) After the weighting device has been attached, the piece should be operated to recheck high- and low-trim positions.

D.   Removing Loads

The first step in removing a load from a hemp set is to be sure that the stage area underneath is clear. With the lines tied off at high trim, remove the jack line, sandbags, and sunday (or trim clamp) from the rope. Untie the low trim. Sort out the rope, and be sure that it is free and clear. Untie the high trim, keeping a sufficient number of wraps around the pin to maintain control as the flown piece is lowered to the stage floor (figure 3.49).

The friction of the rope around the pin acts as a brake. It is good

3.49 Letting in an unweighted piece

practice never to unwrap the rope completely from the pin until the load is on the floor.

E. Trim Marks

Trim heights on hemp rigging may be marked on the rope by using tape. However, tape can come off or leave a sticky residue when it is removed.

Another method is to use a piece of brightly colored yarn or ribbon. Untwist the rope slightly using a splicing fid or marlinespike and insert a piece of yarn or ribbon about 6" long through the rope. As with tape, different colors can be used to indicate different trim positions (figure 3.50).

F. Lashing with Small Stuff

When tying off high and low trims on different pins, it sometimes helps to use a small cord to lash the low-trim tie-off in place (figure 3.51). Doing so helps keep the lines from fouling on the low-trim pins when moving the piece from high to low trim. The small cord also serves as a reminder not to untie the low-trim pins.

3.50 Yarn trim mark

3.51 Tie-off lashed to pin

G. Retrimming

Because of the effect of moisture on Manila rope, changes in humidity affect the trim of hemp rigging. On multiple-line sets, the
longest ropes undergo the greatest change. Therefore, trims
should always be checked before performance time.

   If a multiple-line set is out of trim, the sunday must be removed
to retrim. If a jack line is being used, the weight of the sandbags
can be tied off with the jack line, thus allowing retrimming without
removing the sunday completely. This is a time-consuming task
and points to the advantage of using a trim clamp. Be sure to
relevel dead-tied sets, as well as those that move.

H. Coiling and Dressing

The extra rope on a fly floor should always be properly coiled and
hung on a pin. This is called *dressing* the rope and keeps the rope
from getting tangled and dirty from the riggers walking on it.

   Keep the fly floor clean so that, when rope is placed on the floor,
it will not get dirty. (See section 3.03.G-4.)

I. Showtime Operation

Operating rigging during a performance is very much like stage
managing. Most of the work is in the preparation, well before the
performance. Knowing the rigging system, being sure that it is in
good, safe condition, properly attaching the loads, clearly setting
trim marks, and properly dressing the loose rope on the fly floor all
contribute to an organized and reliable performance. It is good practice to check trim marks and low-trim tie-offs before every performance. Be sure the trim marks are still in place. Be sure that tie-
offs have not slipped and that humidity has not changed rope
lengths.

   When letting a piece in, check the load first by pulling on the
standing part of the line; then remove the coiled rope from the pin
and lay it on the fly floor. It should be placed where it cannot be
stepped on, so that the rope will uncoil evenly, without tangling.

   On the "warn" cue, find the proper rope and review which direction it moves. On the "standby" cue, untie (if it is being let in) or get
ready to pull (if it is being taken out). On the "go" cue, move the
piece, being sure that either the operator or the spotter can see
the piece and the stage floor under it.

3.10   Operation Summary

1. Know the rigging system. Know it well enough to detect any abnormality during operation.
2. Inspect the system thoroughly at regular intervals.
3. Be sure to use an adequate design factor for the degree of risk involved.
4. Use the correct knots for attaching loads and tying off on the pin rail.
5. Maintain visual contact with a moving piece, using a spotter if necessary.
6. Warn people on the stage and the grid before moving a flown piece.
7. Maintain control of a moving piece at all times.
8. Wear hand protection.
9. Keep the working area clean.

3.11   Safety-Inspection Summary

On a regular basis, at least once a year, the rigging system should have a thorough safety inspection. This service can be provided by professional rigging companies for a fee. The inspection should include:

1. Rope: (*a*) inspect the entire length of each rope; (*b*) inspect the alignment and fleet angle of each rope.
2. Pin rail: (*a*) inspect the mounting bolts that hold the rail down; (*b*) smooth rough spots on wooden rails.
3. Head and loft blocks: (*a*) inspect and tighten mounting clamps; (*b*) check support steel for deflection; (*c*) check for dry bearings.
4. Sandbags: check for rot, tears, deterioration.
5. Trim clamps and sundays: check general condition.

3.12   Historical Summary

This type of rigging has been in use since Western theatre was founded by the ancient Greeks as a part of their religious festivals. Some of the plays by Aeschylus, Euripides, and Aristophanes require characters to fly through the air. Since these theatres were open to the sky and had no grids, this effect was accomplished by a device called the *machina*. Because the most commonly flown characters were gods, the device became known later as the *deus ex machina*—God in the machine.

The *machina* was a device consisting of a rope drawn through a series of pulleys, which were mounted on a pivoting boom. The boom, in turn, was mounted on top of the *skena*—or stage house. A person or object could be lifted from, or lowered onto, the stage by stagehands working the offstage end of the rope. The boom could be rotated to move the flown object onstage or offstage.

It is generally believed that the technology that made this possible was adapted from that used by Greek sailors. Then, as now, rigging required a good knowledge of the care and use of rope, as well as the ability to tie knots properly.

Today's theatres are generally enclosed structures; many of them have grids; many of them have complex, sophisticated systems for flying stage effects. But still commonly found in use is the simple technique of fastening an object to a rope, running the rope through pulleys, and raising the object into the air. There are many variations and combinations of hemp-rigging systems, but hemp remains the most basic of all stage rigging. To be a competent stage technician, it is essential to know the correct use of hemp rigging.

Part 4   Counterweight Rigging

4.01   Introduction

The invention of counterweight rigging was the next logical step in the progression of flying equipment for the stage. It began to appear in the first quarter of the twentieth century. The early systems employed a rack, or arbor, in which to stack metal weights. This arbor was attached to the hemp lift lines, and a single hand line was attached to the arbor. The shrinking and stretching of the hemp lift lines, because of changes in humidity, still posed a problem. This was solved by using a wire rope for the lift lines (lead lines). Wire guides gave the arbors some vertical stability. Eventually, T-bar guide rails appeared and have become the most common form of guide system.

  For efficiency, the counterweight system is a great improvement over hemp rigging. The onstage load can be counterweighted much faster than one can bag a hemp set. The single hand line, wire-rope lift lines, and lock rail reduce work and thus save time.

4.02 Single-Purchase Counterweight System

A typical single-purchase counterweight set (see figure 4.1) consists of:

1. Head block for lift line and hand line
2. Loft blocks (mule blocks as needed)
3. Wire-rope lift lines
4. Batten
5. Hand line (purchase line)
6. Counterweight arbor
7. Lock rail
8. Tension block
9. T-bar guide rails
10. Loading bridge

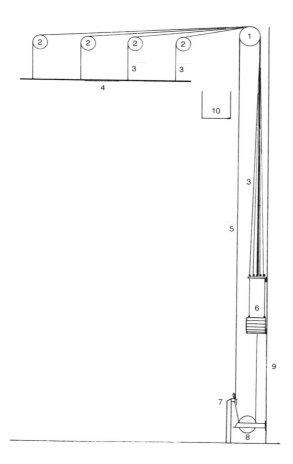

**4.1
Single-purchase
counterweight set**

This system is used when there is clear wall space on one side of the stage from grid height to the stage floor.

Counterweights are used in a 1:1 ratio; that is, 1 lb of counterweight is needed for each pound of load weight.

4.03 Double-Purchase Counterweight System

A double-purchase system is used when some obstruction prevents full travel of the arbor from grid to stage floor. Note the compound rigging of both hand line and lift line in figure 4.2. The batten travels 2′ for every 1′ of travel for the arbor. Consequently, 2 lb of counterweight are required for every 1 lb of load.

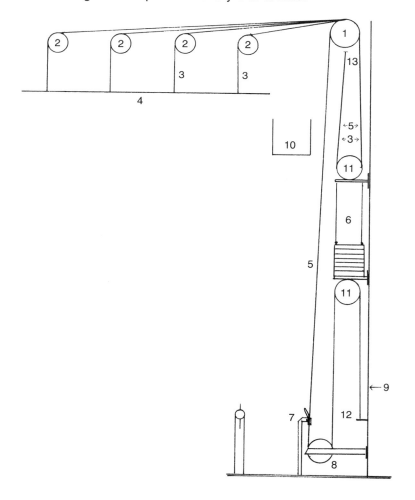

**4.2
Double-purchase
counterweight set**

The arbors must be sized larger than in a single-purchase system for it to have the same lifting capacity. Larger arbors often make loading and unloading more difficult and thus more dangerous. Quite often 2 loading bridges are required to safely load the longer arbors.

A typical double-purchase counterweight system (see figure 4.2) consists of:

1. Head block for lift line and hand line
2. Loft blocks (mule blocks as needed)
3. Wire-rope lift lines
4. Batten
5. Hand line
6. Counterweight arbor
7. Lock rail
8. Tension block
9. T-bar guide rails
10. Loading bridge
11. Arbor blocks
12. Hand line tie-off
13. Hand line and lift line tie-off

4.04   Miscellaneous Hardware

Knowing the rigging system includes knowing the capacity of every part of a system. A line set is only as strong as the weakest piece of hardware in it, and this includes the miscellaneous hardware: wire-rope clips, swage fittings, shackles, pear rings, chain, and other items used for rigging purposes but not made by manufacturers of theatrical rigging hardware. When using this type of hardware for rigging applications, you should use only hardware with a manufacturer's name and load, or application, rating on it and, if possible, a *Product Identification Code* (PIC).

When a manufacturer places its name on a product, it means that it is willing to stand behind that product. It guarantees that it will do the job for which it is designed. The companies that manufacture this type of hardware have engineering departments that are willing to answer your questions about the use and application of their products.

Shackles, pear rings, chain, and other load-bearing products generally have a rated working load limit. This is a percentage of the ultimate breaking strength, well below the yield point of the material from which it is made (see section 1.06.C). Many manufacturers put the design factor for the particular item in their catalog, simplifying the task of increasing the design factor in case of great risk when using these products.

The PIC includes the year the product was manufactured, the plant where it was manufactured, and the heat number of the metal used for that particular item. The PIC, along with the manufacturer's name, assures the user of complete traceability in case of component failure and the manufacturer's liability for the quality of its product.

By purchasing hardware that has only the country of origin stamped on it, you place all of the liability on the user. It is impossible to trace the product in case of failure. Many of the imported hardware items have a working load limit stamped on them, but there is no catalog information indicating the design factor. In fact, the design factor may be only 1:1 or 2:1, while a comparable U.S. product may be 4:1 or 5:1. With only a country of origin on the product, there is no catalog to consult or engineer to call for further information. A country obviously will not assume any liability if the piece of hardware fails.

4.05   Wire Rope

With the invention of the counterweight rigging system, wire rope replaced hemp as the lift line material. Wire rope is not susceptible to stretching or shrinking from humidity changes, and it is much stronger per unit of cross-sectional area than Manila rope. Many types of wire rope are manufactured for industrial applications, and not one is designed specifically for theatrical use. Although several types of wire rope have been used for rigging over the years, some are more appropriate than others. The specific properties and types are discussed below.

A.   Properties of Wire Rope for Stage Rigging

1. Reserve Strength

The outer wires of a wire rope are subject to wear and abrasion, while the inner wires are protected. The *reserve strength* is the ratio of outer wires and inner wires to the total metallic area. The more inner metallic area in relation to the outer metallic area, the greater the reserve strength. This property is of great interest to the elevator and crane industries, where a certain number of broken outer wires are allowed before the wire rope needs to be replaced. It is of less significance for rigging applications. For stage rigging, however, even *one* broken wire is cause to replace the wire rope immediately.

2. Flexibility

Wire rope, when used for stage rigging, is constantly being bent over sheaves and cable drums. Repeated bending and straightening requires a flexible and fatigue-resistant type of wire rope. Preforming the wire into a helix before twisting it into strands reduces internal friction and increases flexibility.

The smaller the diameter of each wire, the more flexible the wire rope. Choosing a wire rope with a greater number of wires per cross-sectional area increases flexibility and fatigue resistance. Wire rope is made of many pieces of wire. Bending a piece of wire back and forth will eventually fatigue it until it breaks. (See section 1.06.F-1.) This is true for wire rope as well. Constant bending will eventually fatigue the wires in the rope until they break. The number of repeated bends before failure is called the *fatigue life cycle* of the wire rope. The greater the fatigue resistance, the longer it will last.

a. D/d ratio. The ratio of the sheave tread diameter (D) to the wire-rope diameter (d) is called the D/d ratio. The larger the D/d ratio, the less sharp the bend over the sheave and the longer the cable will resist fatigue failure. (See section 4.06.B.)

b. Reverse bending. Reverse bending can reduce the life of a wire rope by as much as 50%. When installing new wire rope, take it off the spool carefully and install it so that its major direction of bending is in the same direction as it was on the spool.

It is not always possible to avoid reverse bending. Figure 3.24 shows wire rope being subjected to reverse bends by mule blocks. If an installation requires reverse bending of the wire rope, try to place the blocks as far apart as possible and use as large a sheave as reasonable. The reverse bends will shorten the fatigue life cycle of the wire rope, thus requiring more frequent inspection.

3. Abrasion Resistance

In normal operation, a wire rope is subjected to surface abrasion. Excessive fleet angles and the absence of sag bars and idler pulleys contribute to abrasive wear. The larger in diameter the outer wires are, the more the metal can wear away before the wire breaks. Larger diameter wires generally mean greater abrasive resistance.

Another factor in abrasion resistance is the grade of the wire rope. The grade refers to the metal from which the wire rope is made. The chemical content of the steel determines the abrasion resistance and strength for a given diameter wire. Generally, the stronger the grade of wire rope, the more abrasion resistant it is.

For outdoor applications, where the wire rope is being dragged over the ground, abrasion resistance is very important. For normal theatrical use, it is one of the properties that must be balanced against the others in selecting the proper wire rope for the job.

4. Size

When wire rope is manufactured, its diameter is slightly oversized. After a load is applied, it stretches, and the individual wires seat themselves closer to each other, thus slightly reducing the diameter. This stretching is called *construction stretch.* See section 6.02.C for the effect on termination devices.

There are federal specifications that pertain to the plow steel and aircraft-cable categories of wire rope. The allowable diameter tolerances in these specifications for domestic wire rope permit a variance of –0% +5%, thus never allowing the wire rope to be undersize, yet allowing the wire rope to be slightly oversize, even after construction stretch.

Imported wire rope is based on metric sizing and is adapted for U.S. use. The current metric tolerances are –1% +4%, thus allowing the imported wire rope to be slightly undersize. There is a movement afoot to change the metric tolerances to the same as those in the U.S.

Any difference in diameter causes a difference in strength. The tensile strength of a material is dependent on its cross-sectional area. A smaller-diameter wire rope of similar construction and material has less cross-sectional area, thus less strength, than one of larger diameter.

5. Strength

Strength is a major factor in selecting a type of wire rope for a rigging application. Wire-rope strength is stated in terms of ultimate breaking strength. (See section 1.06.) The type of material denoted by the grade determines the strength of the wire rope for a given diameter. (See section 4.05.C.) Wire rope should never be stressed beyond the yield point. For this reason, *a minimum design factor for running wire rope used for theatrical purposes is 8:1.* That is, the maximum allowable load is ⅛ the breaking strength. As the degree of risk increases, the design factor must also increase. This design factor allows for the fatigue and abrasion of the wire rope.

For slings or other *static* applications, a minimum design factor of 5:1 is used. The degree of fatigue and abrasion is much less for static applications.

B. Construction of Wire Rope

Wire rope is made of many wires twisted together in various combinations to provide a strong, flexible cable. There are classifications of the patterns in which the wires are twisted.

1. Core Construction

The *core* is the center of the wire rope around which the outer strands are wrapped. The center is usually one of 3 types: *fiber core* (FC), *independent wire-rope core* (IWRC), or *wire-strand core* (WSC). Wire-strand core is sometimes also abbreviated SC.

The *fiber core* is made of natural or synthetic fiber. It is softer and more flexible than the IWRC and is easier to crush under load. It deforms more under compressive termination devices. Natural-fiber cores retain lubricant, which has been known to leak on the stage. They are also weaker than IWRC wire ropes. Plow steel wire ropes are available with an FC.

Independent wire-rope core is a separate wire rope around which the outer strands are wrapped. It resists crushing and is less flexible and stronger than a fiber-core wire rope. Galvanized aircraft cable greater than ⅜" in diameter has an IWRC. Plow steel wire ropes are available with IWRC.

Wire-strand cores have the same construction as the outer strands of a wire rope. Galvanized aircraft cable below ⅜" has a WSC.

2. Classification

Wire rope is classified according to the number of wires and strands. For example, in a 7 X 19 classification, the first number (7) denotes the number of strands; the second number (19) denotes the number of wires in each strand. Typical classifications are 6 X 19, 6 X 37, and 7 X 19.

Plow steels for stage use are made in the 6 X category. The number of wires per strand varies, giving the user a wide choice of flexibility and abrasion resistance. There are 2 broad construction classifications for plow steel, 6 X 19 and 6 X 37. Within the 6 X 19 classification, there are wire ropes with 19 through 26 wires in each strand. Within the 6 X 37 category, there are wire ropes with 36 to 49 wires per strand (figure 4.3). Wire ropes with the same di-

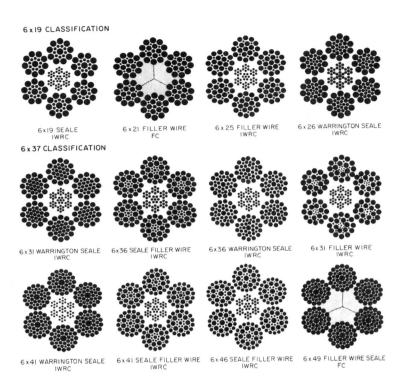

6 x 19 CLASSIFICATION

6 x 19 SEALE
IWRC

6 x 21 FILLER WIRE
FC

6 x 25 FILLER WIRE
IWRC

6 x 26 WARRINGTON SEALE
IWRC

6 x 37 CLASSIFICATION

6 x 31 WARRINGTON SEALE
IWRC

6 x 36 SEALE FILLER WIRE
IWRC

6 x 36 WARRINGTON SEALE
IWRC

6 x 31 FILLER WIRE
IWRC

6 x 41 WARRINGTON SEALE
IWRC

6 x 41 SEALE FILLER WIRE
IWRC

6 x 46 SEALE FILLER WIRE
IWRC

6 x 49 FILLER WIRE SEALE
FC

4.3 Section drawing of 6 × 19 and 6 × 37 plow steel wire-rope classifications. Courtesy American Iron and Steel Institute, *Wire Rope Users Manual*

4.4 Section drawing of 7 × 19 aircraft cable

ameter, core construction, and grade of wire all have the same breaking strength, regardless of the number of wires per strand.

Aircraft cable most commonly used for theatrical applications is the 7 X 19 classification. The 7th strand is the core (figure 4.4).

C. Grades of Wire Rope

There are many grades of wire rope available. Only those found in theatrical use are discussed here.

1. Plow Steel

Plow steel comes in 4 basic grades: plow steel (PS), improved plow steel (IPS), extra improved plow steel (XIPS), and extra extra improved plow steel (XXIPS). (Once there was a grade called mild plow steel at the very bottom of the strength chart, but it has not been made for quite some time.) Plow steel is a natural-colored steel, usually not galvanized. Each grade increases its strength by approximately 15% from the one below it. PS and IPS grades can be found in older installations and are not readily available anymore. XIPS is generally used today for theatrical applications. XXIPS is available and used for special high-strength applications.

It is impossible to distinguish the different grades of plow steel by eye. They all appear the same. Physical or chemical testing is the only way to differentiate among the various grades. To field test a piece of plow steel wire rope to determine its grade, obtain samples of PS, IPS, and XIPS in the same diameter that you want to test. Cut all samples by hand using a cable cutter. There will be a noticeable difference in the amount of force required to make the cuts. The plow steel will cut very easily. The XIPS will require the most effort, and the IPS will fall in the middle. Cut the unknown sample and compare the force required to the known samples. The 15% strength differential is very noticeable; one cut is usually all that is needed to make a determination. If the unknown sample is harder to cut than the known samples, it probably is XXIPS.

2. Galvanized Aircraft Cable

In recent years, galvanized aircraft cable has become the wire rope of choice for most theatrical work. It is readily available at a reasonable cost and has a good balance of the properties required for theatrical use. Aircraft cable comes in both galvanized and stainless steel. The stainless is less strong and more expensive than the galvanized, and it should only be used where corrosion is a serious problem.

3. Extra Flexible Wire Rope

Applications where the wire rope is subjected to high cycles of operation or a small D/d ratio for sheaves and drums may call for extra flexible wire rope. Extra flexible wire rope is designed to bend over a smaller radius than either plow steel or aircraft cable. It is sold under the trade name 7-Flex by the Macwhyte Corporation.

4. Rotation-Resistant Wire Rope

For applications that require a single lift line that should not rotate,

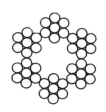

4.5 Section drawing of 6 × 7 sash cord

4.6 Section drawing of 6 × 42 tiller rope

there is a rotation-resistant wire rope available. The directions of twist for the core and outer strands are opposite to each other, giving it a degree of rotational stability.

5. Sash Cord

As the name implies, sash cord is a wire rope for window sashes (figure 4.5). It is made in both a soft iron and a steel version. The soft iron often has a copper coating to resist rust. It is made in a 6 X 7 design, has a fiber core, is extremely soft, and is very weak. There are many old theatres with this wire rope on the counterweight sets. Because of its softness and low strength, it does not take shock loads well and should not be used for theatrical applications.

6. Tiller Rope

Tiller rope is made in a 6 X 42 configuration, has a fiber core, and is usually copper coated (figure 4.6). It is also made in both steel and iron wire and designed for controlling the tillers on small boats. This wire rope has very low strength, low abrasion resistance, and should not be used for theatrical lifting applications.

7. Strength Comparison

The following listing (from the Macwhyte Corporation Catalog G-18) is a comparison of the breaking strength of various types of ¼" wire rope.

Type	Breaking Strength
Sash cord, bright	2,040 lb
Tiller rope, plow steel	2,620 lb
Plow steel IWRC	4,780 lb
Improved plow steel IWRC	5,480 lb
Extra improved plow steel IWRC	6,800 lb
Galvanized aircraft cable	7,000 lb

8. Wire rope for Theatrical Use

When taking over the responsibility for the rigging equipment in an existing facility, one of the first orders of business should be to inspect the rigging equipment. This includes finding out what type and grade of wire rope is being used. Determine if there is more than one type. Look at the physical appearance of the outside of the wire rope. Is it plain metal colored, copper colored, or galvanized? Determine, if possible, the approximate year the wire rope was installed. Open up an end and determine the type of core. Count the number of wires in a strand. Compare what you see to the information found in a good wire-rope catalog. Galvanized aircraft cable, tiller rope, and sash cord are easily identified. Plow steel, because of its various grades, is more difficult and may require a destructive test to determine the grade. If possible, contact the company responsible for installing the rigging system; it may be able to help you answer questions.

Once you determine the type and grade of the wire rope, make a written record of it for future use.

9. Purchasing New Wire Rope

Determine the design load for the line set and the type of use with regard to fatigue, flexibility, and abrasion. Ordinary counterweight sets and many winch sets can use galvanized aircraft cable or 6 X 19 XIPS with an IWRC. If the line set will require a high number of cycles per day, will have excessive reverse bends, or has a small D/d ratio, use a more flexible XIPS, such as 6 X 25 or 6 X 37. If the wire rope is for a permanent installation and a special application, other than a counterweight set, seek a knowledgeable person to help with the selection. Most often, the salesperson at the wire-rope store has no understanding of theatrical requirements. Talk to a theatrical consultant or to a stage equipment company.

When ordering, specify the diameter, breaking strength, core type, number of strands and wires, and grade. Ask for a certified test report of the exact size and breaking strength. There can be a strength difference between domestic and imported wire rope. File the report and a record of the installation date and line sets for which the wire rope was used.

D. Attaching to Batten and Arbor

Applying a load to wire rope causes it to stretch. Even if a batten is evenly loaded, the load on each lift line is not equal. Many loads are not evenly distributed, which adds to the problem of uneven cable stretch. (See section 3.04.A-2.) Therefore, when terminating the lift lines at arbor and batten, a method of adjustment must be provided. The adjustment device can be attached either to the batten end or to the arbor end of the wire rope. Leveling the batten

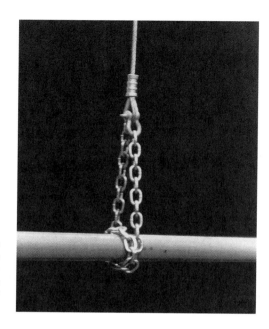

4.7 Lift line attached to batten with trim chain, shackle through eye of wire rope

is much easier if the trimming device is attached to the batten rather than to the arbor. The batten is lowered to a point where it is convenient to measure from floor to batten. Measurements are made where each lift line is attached to the batten, and the lines are lengthened or shortened as required. If the adjusting device is on the arbor, then one person onstage must yell to the person adjusting at the arbor. This is often awkward and time-consuming.

1. Trim Chain

The wire rope is terminated at the end of a chain using a thimble with cable clips or a Nicopress sleeve. In considering the method of terminating the cable, keep in mind that Nicopress sleeves make a termination 95% to 100% efficient. (See section 6.02.C-2.) Cable clips provide an 80% efficient termination. (See section 6.02.C.) The chain is wrapped around the batten 1-½ times and is secured back to the thimble using a shackle (figure 4.7). By attaching the shackle back to the wire-rope thimble, the load is distributed between both sides of the chain and the capacity of the trim chain is doubled. (See section 2.03.A.) If the shackle is attached to a link in the chain, all of the load is on a single link and the point of greatest stress is that link (figure 4.8).

Chain manufacturers recommend that only grade 8 (or better) alloy chain be used for overhead lifting. Alloy chain takes shock load-

4.8 Lift line attached to batten with trim chain, shackle through link of chain, safety bolt through links of chain

ing and stretches before it breaks. Regular steel chain is brittle and will have a tendency to shatter under the stress of a shock load. The problem with grade 8 chain is finding attachment hardware that works with it. On counterweight rigging, the elasticity of the wire rope, as well as its attachment to an arbor that is held in place with a fiber hand line, provides a shock-absorbing system that greatly reduces the shock load on a trim chain.

Until about 10 years ago, 2/0 and 4/0 passing-link chain was often used for trim chains. The 2/0 has a working load limit of about 450 lb, 4/0 of 600 lb, and both with a design factor of 4:1. As loads on counterweight sets began to increase, installers started using ¼" proof coil chain with a working load limit of about 1,300 lb. By attaching both ends of the chain to the wire-rope thimble, the WLL of the chain is 2,600 lb. Based on a 4:1 design factor, the ultimate breaking strength of the double chain is 10,400 lb, which is greater than the breaking strength of the strongest ¼" wire rope.

Snap hooks are often used to secure a trim chain (figure 4.9). However, they are unrated pieces of hardware and should not be used; replace them with appropriately sized shackles. A quick temporary fix can be made by inserting a grade 5 bolt with a grade 5

4.9 Broken snap hook on trim chain on arbor

lock nut in the links below the snap hook as a backup device as shown in figure 4.8.

Quick Links are also used with trim chains. They depend on being fully closed for their strength. Because Quick Links (figure 4.10) can come open as a result of vibration, they are not dependable devices and should not be used for rigging. Most of them do not bear a manufacturer's name, and the design factor is unknown. Shackles from a known manufacturer are a safer choice.

2. Clove Hitch with Wire-Rope Clips

A clove hitch with wire-rope clips is a holdover termination technique from hemp rigging. The wire rope is tied around the batten with a clove hitch, just as fiber rope is. To secure the hitch, the dead end is fastened to the standing part with the recommended number of wire-rope clips (figure 4.11). Destructive testing has shown that the weak point is just above the top clip. The wire rope breaks at this point regardless of how many clips are used. This is the point where all of the support of the load transfers from both halves of the line to just the live line. It is the point of greatest

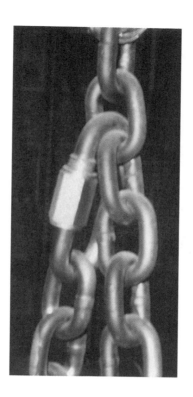

4.10 Loose Quick Link on trim chain

stress on the line at the batten end. From the top clip downward, the load is equally divided between both halves of the line. The clove hitch supports the load on both the lines and is not the weak point of the termination. The efficiency of this termination is 80%, the same as wire-rope clips.

3. Twisted Sash Cord

In the early days of counterweight systems, 6 X 7 sash cord was often used for the wire-rope lift lines. As mentioned in section 4.05.C-5, this is a very weak wire rope and should not be used for stage rigging. It was often tied in a clove hitch around the batten with the dead end wrapped around the standing part. The end was taped to hold it in place. This type of termination places a concentrated stress area right where the standing part of the line makes the first bend of the clove hitch. The photograph in figure 4.12 shows an existing system where the rigger has replaced the tape with two cable clips: this does nothing to strengthen the termination. The entire load is still on the standing part of the line. If the dead end of the line were straight, as in figure 4.11, and the clips

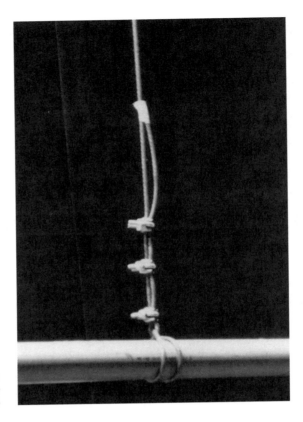

were applied, the load would be shared by both parts of line up to the top clip. Because the dead end of the line is twisted around the live line, it does not support any of the load. In this case, the efficiency of the termination when first applied is that of a clove hitch, about 75%. Due to fatigue and shock loading over time, the wire rope will become deformed at the stress point of the clove hitch, and the termination will become even less efficient.

4. Turnbuckle

The wire rope can be attached to the end of a turnbuckle using a thimble with cable clips or a compression sleeve. Use a turnbuckle with either jaw or eye ends, or a combination of both. Attach the wire rope or batten clamp to an eye with a shackle. Do not fasten the cable directly to the eye. The turnbuckle may need to be replaced, and using a shackle makes replacement easier. A jaw end can be attached directly to the arbor, pipe clamp on the batten, or wire-rope thimble.

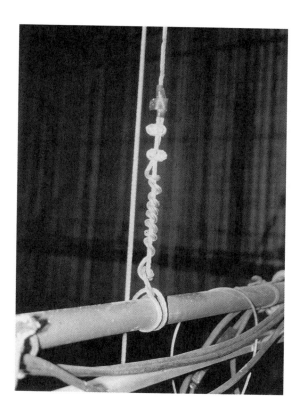

**4.12 Clove hitch
with twisted dead
end of wire rope;
added clips of
little value**

As wire rope runs over a sheave, the twist in the wire rope
causes it to spin. Cotter pins, or No. 12 solid-core electric wire,
through the rod ends or wire mousing should be used to keep the
turnbuckle from turning and separating. Jam nuts do not hold. They
keep the rod of the turnbuckle from closing but not from opening.
All 3 methods are shown in figure 4.13.

E.   Indications of Wear

When inspecting the lift lines for signs of wear, look for broken
wires, flattened wires, separation in wire or strand, rust, signs of
chemical etching, or anything unusual. Wire rope in good condition
is clean, well formed, and free of dirt, grease, and other discolora-
tion (figure 4.14).

In particular, look closely at the wire rope next to the cable clips
and compression fittings. These are points of stress concentrations
and the most likely places to find broken wires caused by overload-

4.13 Turnbuckle on a batten with 2 types of mousing and jam nuts

4.14 Signs of wear and misuse. Courtesy American Iron and Steel Institute, *Wire Rope Users Manual*

ing. An elongated thimble is a sign of excessive stress (figure 4.15). Check terminations very thoroughly.

To check for broken wire over a long run, hold a piece of terry cloth or cotton batting in a gloved hand. Wrap the material gently around the wire rope and have someone operate the line set. The broken wires will snag the material. If using a bare hand instead of fabric, you will follow the bloody trail back to a piece of skin snagged in the broken wire.

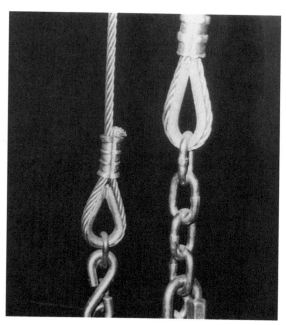

4.15 Regular and deformed thimbles

4.06   Wire-Rope Blocks

In this section, characteristics that pertain specifically to wire-rope blocks are discussed. (For general information pertaining to blocks, see section 3.04.)

A.   Material

The sheaves for wire-rope blocks can be made from a variety of materials; the most common is cast iron. Each material has a finite amount of force that it can withstand before it fails. This force is referred to as *radial pressure*. The radial pressure is dependent on the diameter of the wire rope (d), the load (L), and the tread diameter of the sheave (D). The formula for calculating the radial pressure (*RP*) is:

$$RP = (2 \times L) \div (D \times d)$$

The allowable radial pressure for common sheave materials with 6 X 19 or 7 X 19 wire rope is

Material	Radial Pressure
Cast iron	480 lb
Cast carbon steel	900 lb
Chilled cast iron	1,100 lb
Manganese steel	2,400 lb
Molded Nylatron	700 lb
Cast Nylatron	2,500 lb

The Nylatron figures vary by manufacturer depending on molding patterns and machining techniques. Figure 4.16 shows the effect of excessive radial pressure on a sheave. This kind of scoring causes excessive wear on the wire rope. Eventually the sheave will wear to the point of catastrophic failure.

B. Sizing

Proper sheave-diameter sizing is far more critical for wire rope than for hemp rope. The recommended sheave diameter is a multiple of the wire-rope diameter, called the D/d ratio. (See section 4.05.A-2a.) The minimum sheave tread diameter for 7 X 19 aircraft cable and 6 X 19 wire rope is 30 times the diameter of the wire rope. Us-

4.16 Sheave scored by excessive radial pressure

ing ¼" for example, .25 × 30 = 7.5" minimum sheave tread diameter. The groove of the sheave must also be properly sized for the wire rope. If it is too big, it does not support the wire rope properly, and the wire rope will flatten out and lose strength. If the groove is too small, the abrasion of the cable, rubbing the groove walls, will cause wear on both cable and sheave. A tolerance of −.00" to +.015" is acceptable. Using hemp blocks for wire rope is *never* acceptable.

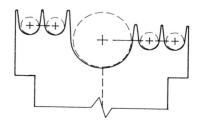

4.17 Section of head block sheave showing equal pitch diameter on right, unequal on left

C. Head Blocks

The head blocks for counterweight sets are grooved for the wire-rope lift lines and the fiber-rope hand line. The pitch diameters for the fiber and wire ropes must be equal, or the hand line and lift lines will run at different speeds. Figure 4.17 shows equal pitch diameter for the hand line and the wire rope. Unequal pitch diameter causes the hand line to slip in the groove of the head block, thus causing wear to the hand line and additional friction in the system. This slippage can often be felt when running the line set. Because friction is a percentage of applied force, the heavier the load, the greater the amount of friction and the greater the effort required to operate the line set. Unequal pitch diameter can only be fixed by replacing the head block sheave or having it remachined.

When inspecting the head blocks, check to see that the lift lines are not crossed, that the fleet angle of all lines is acceptable, and that the clamps are tight and against the support steel. All head block mounting bolts should, at a minimum, be grade 5. (See section 6.03.)

D. Tension Block

The tension block (figure 4.18), found on a single-purchase counterweight set, serves 2 functions. First, because it can *float* (move up and down), it can reduce strain on the hand line as increased

4.18 Tension block

humidity shrinks the rope. Most types of tension pulleys require a downward pressure on the front edge before they can move up on the T-bar guides.

Second, the tension pulley allows the operator to put slack in the hand line in order to put a safety twist in it while loading or unloading. (See section 4.11.A-1.) The tension block guides can become bent from the force generated by doing this. Inspect the guides at regular intervals (figure 4.19).

4.07   Lock Rail

The lock rail is a metal rail with a rope lock for the hand line of each counterweight set. The rope lock (figure 4.20) is intended to keep the batten in a given position under a nearly balanced load condition. THE ROPE LOCK IS NEVER INTENDED TO HOLD A HEAVILY UNBALANCED LOAD WHILE LOADING OR UNLOADING. The lock rail must be firmly anchored to the floor to withstand upthrust and side load applied by stagehands climbing on it. The common upthrust design load is 500 lb per foot.

A.   Lock

The lock consists of a pair of jaws and a hand-operated lever arm. The lever arm has a cam on the side that presses against the on-

4.19 Bent tension block guide

4.20 Rope locks

stage jaw, forcing it against the rope, thus holding the rope between the 2 jaws. A steel ring, which is threaded through the hand line, slips over the lever when it is in the *up,* or locked, position. This ring locks the handle closed and keeps the handle from accidentally falling open. When properly adjusted, the rope lock should be *self-locking*; that is, when the handle goes up 2° past the vertical position, it should stay in position. There is a noticeable feel when the cam on the handle goes over the center and into position.

B. Lock Adjustment

The pressure of the jaws is designed to be easily adjusted by turning the thumbscrew on the back side of the lock (figure 4.21). Missing thumbscrews should be replaced immediately. If the handle cannot be adjusted to be self-locking, the cam on the handle or the onstage jaw is worn out and must be replaced.

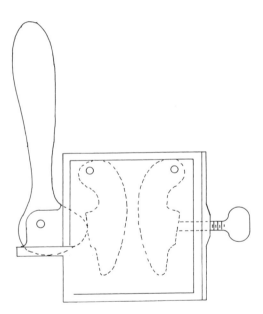

4.21 Rope lock detail

C. Load Limit and Identification

The lock rail is a good place to mark the load limit of each rigging set, as well as to identify each set by number and purpose. Rigging sets are numbered from downstage to upstage.

4.08   Arbor

The *arbor* is the rack that holds the counterweights. It consists of a top plate, a bottom plate, a steel back plate, 2 guide shoe assemblies, and 2 steel rods ¾" in diameter. Wire guide systems do not have the guide shoe assemblies and often do not have back plates. Steel plates, called *spreader plates* or *spreader bars*, slide on the rods. Top plates have collars and thumbscrews and are called *lock plates*. As weights are stacked on the arbor, the spreader bars should be distributed every 2′ to 3′. In the event the counterweight set moves too fast and the arbor slams into the top or bottom stops, the spreader plates keep the rods from bending so the counterweights do not fall out.

The lock plate should always be used on top of the counterweights. Its function is to keep the counterweights from falling out of the arbor in case of a crash. It can only do this if it is in place and the thumbscrews are tight (figure 4.22). Figure 4.23 shows how *not* to use the spreader plates. *Lock and spreader plates are like seat belts; you only need to have them in place at the moment of impact. Since you cannot know when the moment of impact will be, you need to use them all the time.* CAUTION: If the arbor tops and bottoms are cast iron, inspect them carefully and frequently for cracks.

A.   Guide Systems

There are two types of guide systems for arbors. The simplest and noisiest is a wire guide system (figure 4.24). These generally should not be used for line sets with more than 35′ of travel. No matter how tight the guide wires are, it is impossible to keep the arbor from swinging side to side. If they are used for systems with greater travel distances, the line sets should be spaced far enough apart so the arbors do not hit each other.

Periodically, check the wires to see that they are tight and that they are not worn. CAUTION: *Do not overtighten the guide wires.* Overtightening can bend the support steel to which the ends are fastened, whether they are part of the building or part of the head block.

The other type of guide system for arbors is a track system, most commonly called a *T-bar* guide system. The name is derived from the shape of the guide rails (figure 4.25).

The arbor has guide shoes, or rollers, that run on the rails. If the arbor becomes hard to move, check the guide and T-bars for

**4.22
Counterweights
with spreader
and lock plates
in place**

proper alignment. The guide shoes may need replacement. *Never grease the T-bar*. The grease will attract dust and dirt, and it will ultimately make the arbor even harder to move.

B. Pipe Weight

Most of the time, enough weight is left on the arbor to balance the batten weight. This is called the *pipe weight*. It is good practice to paint these weights a distinctive color to aid the loaders when they are taking weights off the arbor.

NOTE: The spreader plates are *not* intended to mark pipe weight. Using them to mark pipe weights keeps them out of the way when loading and unloading the arbor, but is of little help during a runaway.

4.23 How not to use spreader plates

4.24 Wire guide counterweight set

4.25 T-bar guide counterweight set

4.09   Hand Line

Until recently, most hand lines were Manila rope. Nowadays, 3-strand twist and parallel-core polyester have become the ropes of choice. Because Manila changes its length with changes in humidity, it should be adjusted by retying it if it becomes very tight or slack. Sometimes it is necessary to retie polyester after the construction stretch is worked out of it. On single-purchase systems, this is done on the underside of the arbor (figure 4.26).

The arbor is raised and locked off. The knot, usually 2 half hitches, is retied to adjust to the proper tension. Taping the tail of the rope to the hand line keeps it from getting in the way during operation.

On a double-purchase set, one end of the hand line is tied off on the head block beam, and the other is tied off somewhere near the lock rail. Whichever knot is most convenient to reach may be used for adjustment. Since the knot is not moving, no taping is necessary. However, the end of the rope should be taped or whipped to prevent fraying. (See section 6.01.)

4.26 Hand line tied at arbor bottom

On both single- and double-purchase systems, be sure the knot does not interfere with arbor travel.

4.10   Loading Bridge

The loading bridge is the platform where the arbors are loaded and unloaded. A safe loading bridge is placed at a height where the arbors can be easily reached when the battens are 3′ to 5′ above the stage floor. So that the loaders can safely see what they are doing, there should be adequate lighting.

A.   Storing Weights

There should be a kick rail on both edges of the loading bridge to keep the counterweights from being kicked off (figure 4.27). COUNTERWEIGHTS SHOULD NEVER BE STACKED HIGHER THAN THE KICK RAIL! If possible, they should also be stacked on the onstage side of the bridge, so the loaders do not have to walk on them while working.

4.27 Counterweights stored on loading bridge

B. Loading and Unloading Weights

As a rule, two people should work on the loading bridge. One person hands the weights to the other, who loads them on the arbor. To reduce the chance of dropping weights, the transfer of weights is done over the loading bridge, never in the open space next to the arbor. The reverse is done for unloading.

It is easiest for the person loading and unloading to grasp the weights in the middle (figure 4.28). The person handing the weights to the loader should hold them by the ends (figure 4.29).

C. Identifying Load Limits and Weights

It is good practice to post the weight of the variously sized counterweights in some obvious place on the loading bridge. The capacity of the batten can be indicated on the lock plate, the batten, or other convenient locations (figure 4.30).

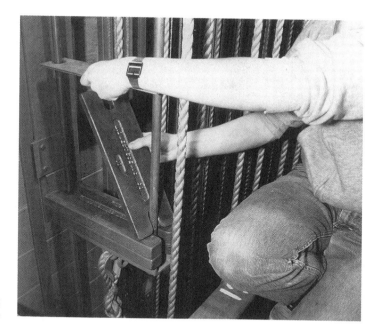

4.28 Loading counterweights

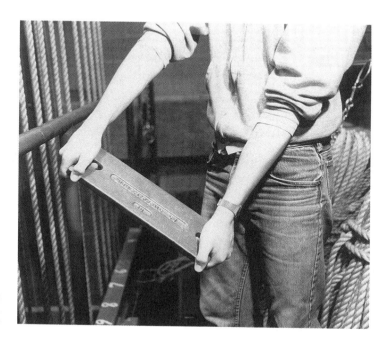

4.29 Handing counterweights to loader

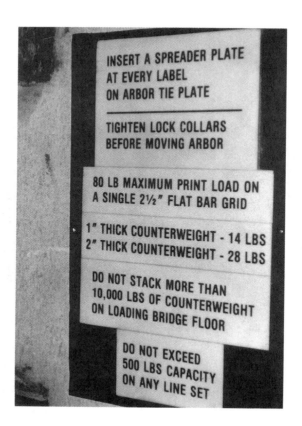

4.30 Sign on loading bridge (should read "Maximum point load . . . ")

The sign reads:

INSERT A SPREADER PLATE
AT EVERY LABEL
ON ARBOR TIE PLATE

TIGHTEN LOCK COLLARS
BEFORE MOVING ARBOR

80 LB MAXIMUM PRINT LOAD ON
A SINGLE 2½" FLAT BAR GRID

1" THICK COUNTERWEIGHT - 14 LBS
2" THICK COUNTERWEIGHT - 28 LBS

DO NOT STACK MORE THAN
10,000 LBS OF COUNTERWEIGHT
ON LOADING BRIDGE FLOOR

DO NOT EXCEED
500 LBS CAPACITY
ON ANY LINE SET

4.11 Loading and Unloading Using a Loading Bridge

Counterweight sets are designed to be used in a balanced condition. This means that the load on the batten is equally balanced with the counterweights on the arbors. During the loading and unloading process, an *unbalanced* condition exists. *This condition is potentially very dangerous!* THE ENTIRE LOADING AND UNLOADING PROCEDURE SHOULD BE HANDLED WITH GREAT CARE. The basic rule for working with an unbalanced load is KEEP THE WEIGHT DOWN: Never depend on the lock or the lock rail to hold weight in the air.

A. Crew Responsibilities

To avoid holding weight in the air, it is essential that a proper loading and unloading sequence be followed. In addition, it is essential that the crews loading weights, working the lock rail, and attaching scenery or lights to the battens thoroughly know their jobs.

1. The Rail Operator

The operator on the lock rail directs the loading and unloading. The operator controls the sequence by giving directions for attaching or removing loads, as well as for adding or removing counterweights. If a heavy show is being set in or taken out, assistant operators control the hand lines while the head operator directs the operation. When loading or unloading, ALWAYS HAVE A SAFETY WRAP ON THE HAND LINE. There is always a chance of the counterweight set becoming unbalanced with the load in the air. Therefore, one of the methods of putting a safety wrap on the line should be used (see figures 4.31–4.38).

Method 1. Twist the hand line. Step down on the front of the tension pulley, and pull up on the back hand line. This will create slack in the hand line. Twist one rope around the other, 4 or 5 times. Apply tension to the front rope by hand (figure 4.31), or place a belaying pin in the ropes for ease in holding (figure 4.32). NEVER RELY ON THE ROPE LOCK TO HOLD AN UNBALANCED LOAD! Twisting the hand line

4.31 Safety twist in hand line

**4.32 Belaying
pin in hand line**

will cause the tension block to pull up in the front, which puts a great deal of strain on the tension block guides and may cause them to bend. (See section 4.06.D.) Once the load is attached and the arbor is loaded, hold onto the front line while keeping the hand lines twisted. Allow the line to slip as the load is raised off of the floor. When the load is clear of the floor, if the load feels balanced, untwist the line and operate normally. If the load is not balanced, pull the arbor to where the weight can be adjusted and do it.

Method 2. Tie a safety hitch from the hand line to the lock rail. In the past, it was common to use a piece of Manila or cotton sash cord to tie off the hand line (figure 4.33). With the introduction of polyester hand line, small-diameter nylon, Spectra, or Kevlar mountain-climbing accessory cord is coming into use (figure 4.34). Spectra and Kevlar are much stronger than nylon. Two knots that work well for attaching the safety line to the hand line are the stopper hitch and the prusik knot (see sections 6.01.B-3–4). The smaller diameter of the synthetic tie-off line grips the synthetic hand line better and gives more secure holding power than Manila. The synthetic line also works well on Manila hand line. Tying off the hand line places all of the stress on the tie-off line and not on the ten-

4.33 Safety hitch on hand line

sion block. This method is the easiest on the tension block guides.

Quite often the load—a piece of scenery or a curtain—will be on the floor after it is attached to the batten. The arbor is weighted, and the line set is out of balance until the load is lifted clear of the floor. If the tie-off is removed while the weight is on the floor, the overweight arbor can run away, jerking the load into the air. Both the stopper hitch and the prusik can be slipped on the hand line, allowing the operator to control the load until it is balanced. Get some help to pull down slightly on the tied-off hand line. When there is a bit of slack on the tie-off line, place your hand on top of

4.34 Prusik knot on synthetic safety line

4.35 Slipping the knot on the safety line

the knot and slide it down the hand line (figure 4.35). Ease the hand line up a bit and continue this process until the load is clear of the floor. Check the balance by pulling on the hand line. If the load is balanced enough to control, remove the tie-off line.

Method 3. Use a Line Lok. I first saw a Line Lok (figures 4.36 and 4.37) in a theatre in Calgary, Canada. Some months later,

4.36 Line Lok

while doing a rigging seminar at the Banff Center, I mentioned the Line Lok. The technical director not only had some in the theatre but gave me the drawing in figure 4.38 to make one. He mentioned that the device first appeared in Canada with a touring U.S. road show. After the first edition of this book was published, I moved to Seattle and found that the device was originally made by a Seattle stagehand. In his honor, it is called an "Uncle Buddy." This is a typical example of how information on rigging is passed along from one place to another in the theatre.

NOTE: The drawing of how to make a Line Lok, or Uncle Buddy, that appeared in the first edition contains a dimensional error and

**4.37 Line Lok on
hand line**

has been corrected in this edition. The original drawing indicates a space from the inside of the hooks to the front of the steel tube of 1". This dimension should be the same as the diameter of the hand line. If manufactured as drawn and used on a line less than 1" in diameter, it could slip. The slack space can be taken up by attaching a plate of the correct thickness on the inside of the tube, as shown in figure 4.37.

Figure 4.39 shows a commercially manufactured device that works in a similar manner. Both devices can be used as a brake to move an unbalanced load, similar to slipping the tie-off knot above. This is done by releasing the bottom hook, placing one hand at the top of the device and rocking the bottom with the other hand.

Method 4. Use a bull line. See section 4.12.B-2.

Method 5. Use a bull or capstan winch. See section 4.12.B-3.

Method 6. Use a block and tackle. See section 4.12.B-4. *Never leave the hand line unattended when a counterweight set is being loaded or unloaded.*

2. Loading Bridge Crew

The loading bridge crew should add or remove weights only when instructed to do so by the rail operator. Adding weight to an arbor

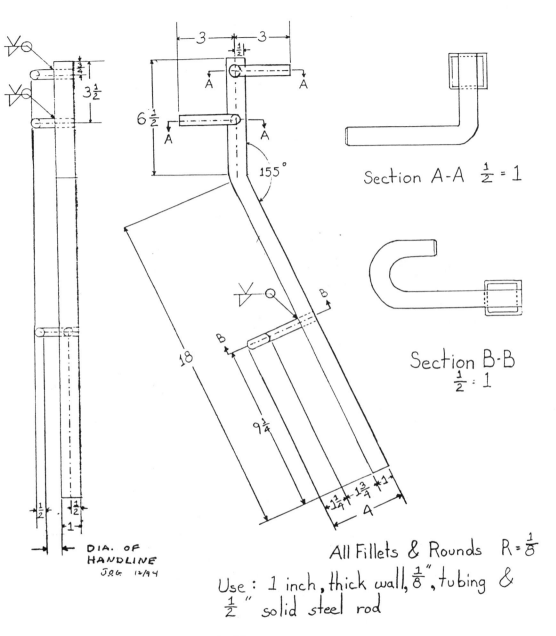

Section A-A $\frac{1}{2}$ = 1

Section B-B $\frac{1}{2}$: 1

155°

18

9$\frac{3}{4}$

DIA. OF
HANDLINE
J.2.G 12/94

All Fillets & Rounds R = $\frac{1}{8}$

Use : 1 inch, thick wall, $\frac{1}{8}$", tubing &
$\frac{1}{2}$" solid steel rod

4.38 Line Lok detail. Courtesy Wes Jenkins

4.39 Commercial line holder

before a load is attached to a batten can cause an unbalanced condition. This could leave the counterweights hanging in the air, supported only by the hand line. Follow safe procedure for loading weights, using spreader bars and lock plates. (See section 4.10.)

3. Stage Crew

The crew onstage attaches the load to the batten. The head carpenter or head electrician supervises batten and spot line loading and unloading. The rail operator gives the order to the stage crew to attach or remove the load. Removing the load from a batten before the arbor is unloaded is dangerous.

When scenery or curtains are resting on the floor while being attached or removed from a batten, their full weight is not offsetting the counterweights needed to balance them. The stage crew may have to hold the batten down as counterweights are being added or removed. They do this either by holding the batten with their hands or by using a bull line. (See section 4.12.B.) WHEN HOLDING A BATTEN BY HAND, NEVER LEAN OVER THE BATTEN. IT MAY BE NECESSARY TO LET GO QUICKLY IF THE BATTEN BEGINS TO RUN AWAY.

B. Communications

The crews onstage, on the loading bridge, and at the lock rail must be able to hear the directions given by the rail operator. If, for any reason, the rail operator has difficulty being heard, electronic voice reinforcement should be used.

There are often many people working on and above the stage. It is important to shout a warning to all before moving a batten in or out. The normal warning is to shout, "heads up," "heads," or "line set No.——— moving." It is also helpful to indicate where the piece is moving (e.g., "Upstage, heads up."). When working on the stage, *never stand or walk under a moving rigging set. Never move a rigging set when someone is under it.*

C. Runaway Set

If crew members involved in loading or unloading a counterweight set lose their concentration, it is possible for them to make a mistake and for the set to become unbalanced and run away. This happens when the weight in the air is so heavy that it cannot be held by the rope lock. If it starts to creep, it may be possible to stop it by brute strength and quickly correct the situation. However, if the set begins to move rapidly, indicating a very heavy out-of-balance condition, DO NOT ATTEMPT TO STOP IT! To do so could cause serious injury. If a runaway should occur, *shout a warning to all crews, and take cover.* Everyone should take cover to protect themselves from flying counterweights and objects falling from the grid.

The arbor will crash either down or up, depending on which part of the line set is heavy; and the chance is great that counterweights and smashed head blocks, tension blocks, or other hardware will fly through the air. The batten will go up or go down, and the possibilities of adjacent flown objects being hit, lift lines snapping, loft blocks smashing and falling, and sprinkler systems being activated are all very real. The only reasonable course of action is to get quickly out of harm's way. RUNAWAYS ARE CAUSED BY HUMAN ERROR. CONCENTRATION ON THE TASK AT HAND IS ESSENTIAL TO USING RIGGING SAFELY.

D. Loading

The loading procedure is as follows:

1. Attach the load to the batten. If a great deal of weight is rest-

ing on the floor, make provision for holding the batten down until the counterweight has been loaded.

2.   Load the counterweight arbor.

3.   Slowly raise the batten to test for balance, keeping it under control at all times.

4.   Add or subtract weight as needed for final balancing.

E.   Unloading

1. Unload weight from the arbor first.
2. Remove weight from the batten.

4.12   Loading and Unloading without a Loading Bridge

Some facilities do not have loading bridges, or the arbors cannot be reached from the loading bridge when the batten is down. This is particularly true with lighting battens. The electric cable cradle often restricts the full travel of the battens and arbor.

A.   Partial Loads

Where it is possible to attach partial loads to the batten, such as with a lighting batten, the procedure is as follows:

1. Put a small amount of weight on the arbor—enough so that the operator can safely raise the arbor to a height where the batten can be reached.

2. Add part of the load to the batten, overloading the batten slightly.

3. Lower the arbor so more weight can be added. This procedure is followed back and forth until both batten and arbor are fully loaded and balanced. Needless to say, the rail operators must be strong and in good physical condition for this work.

4. For unloading, the procedure is reversed. Do not remove all of the load or counterweights at one time. This could result in a runaway set.

B.   Unbalanced Large Loads

Sometimes it is necessary to attach large loads as a single unit. This requires moving either the arbor or the batten with a great deal of weight in an unbalanced condition. While this is difficult, with proper techniques and planning the danger can be minimized. Sufficient force must be used to move the unbalanced load to a point where it can be balanced. Several options are possible.

1. Human Method

Weight permitting, a group of people operate the hand line by brute strength.

4.40 Bull line on a batten

2. Bull Line

A bull line (figure 4.40) can be used on the batten. A bull line is a long piece of rope, ⅝" to ¾" diameter, that is doubled over the batten near one of the lift lines. The stage crew can then pull on this line and aid the operator in raising or lowering an overweight arbor. The line is doubled so that it can be pulled free once the load is balanced. The bull line must be placed near a lift line or the batten can be bent. More than one bull line can be used on a batten.

3. Capstan Winch or Bull Winch

A capstan winch (figure 4.41) is a movable winch that aids in pulling the arbor down or in keeping the arbor from rising too rapidly. A rope is attached to the bottom of the arbor. It is then wrapped several times around the capstan of the winch, and the winch is turned on. Applying tension to the free end of the rope causes it to tighten around the capstan and allows the winch to help move the unbalanced load.

A movable winch with a wire-rope drum is called a *bull winch* (figure 4.42). All of the pulling force is applied by the winch. No pulling by hand on the line is necessary.

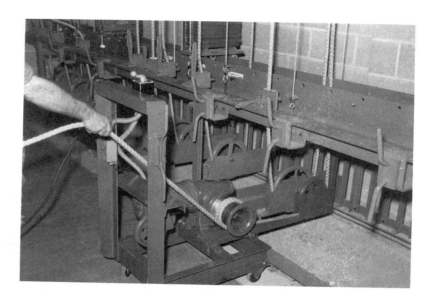

4. Block and Tackle

A block and tackle can be used to raise or lower an unbalanced load. It can be rigged to the head block beam and the top of the arbor to help lift an arbor-heavy load; or it can be rigged to the lock rail and the bottom of the arbor to help raise a batten-heavy load. The fall block can also be attached to the hand line using a sunday with a prusik knot.

5. Sandbag Substitution

When battens are used to store scenery during a performance, there may not be time to unload the arbor when the scenery is removed from the batten. To keep the counterweight set in balance, a sandbag may be moved onstage on a dolly and attached to the batten near one of the lift lines. The weight of the sandbag will compensate for the weight of the removed scenery.

If the weight is heavy, the sandbag must be attached near one of the lift lines, or it will bend the batten. Remember, attach the sandbag before removing the scenery.

6. Carpet Hoist

The carpet hoist (figure 4.43) is also used in situations where the load will be removed from the batten during a performance. To make and use a carpet hoist, do the following:

    a.   Bolt a bracket to the bottom of the arbor.

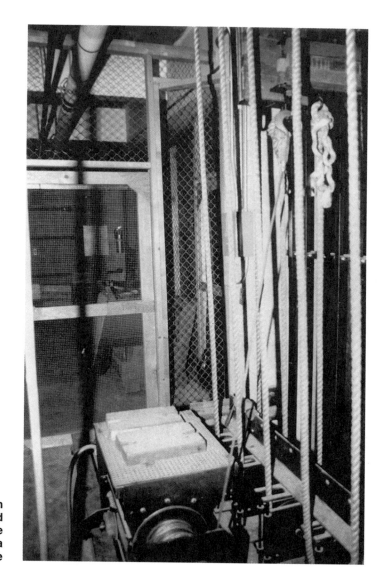

4.42 Bull winch used to load arbor in the absence of a loading bridge

The bracket should extend out from the arbor far enough to prevent the adjacent arbor from passing it. The bracket must be strong and rigid enough to move the scenery arbor without bending or breaking. There are many different types of arbor bottoms in use. It is beyond the scope of this book to try to detail a bracket that would work for each type. The bracket must be designed to support the applied load and not come loose during operation.

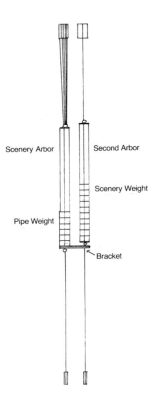

Scenery Arbor

Second Arbor

Scenery Weight

Pipe Weight

Bracket

4.43 Carpet hoist

The bottom of the second arbor rests against the top of the bracket.

- b. The batten and lift lines must be removed from the second arbor.
- c. The scenery arbor is loaded only to pipe weight.
- d. The second arbor is loaded with enough weight to balance the scenery.
- e. To lower the scenery, pull the hand line to raise the scenery arbor.

The weight on the second arbor will follow along and balance the load.

- f. When the scenery is at the point where it will be removed from the batten, lock off the hand line on the second arbor.

Secure a safety hitch between the second arbor hand line and the lock rail. Remove the scenery from the batten. Take the batten out by using the hand line on the scenery arbor.

g. After the scenery is reattached to the batten, release the safety hitch and the rail lock on the second arbor.

Raise the scenery by pulling on the scenery arbor hand line.

NOTE: When the scenery is removed from the batten, the second arbor is out of balance and held in the air by the safety hitch. BE SURE THE HITCH IS WELL TIED. NEVER DEPEND ON THE RAIL LOCK ALONE TO HOLD THE ARBOR! A block and tackle can also be used to hold the second arbor in lieu of the safety hitch. With a sunday, secure the fall block to the hand line that raises the arbor, and secure the standing block to the lock rail. Tie off the lead line to the lock rail to hold the arbor in position.

4.13   Showtime Operation

The reason scenery, curtains, and lights are flown is so that they can be used during a performance. Some flown objects do not move at all, while others move in and out one or more times during a performance. It is essential that you make sure that the flown objects will function as they should for every performance.

A.   Label the Lock Rail

Each counterweight set in use for a production should be clearly labeled on the lock rail. Sets that are storing objects not currently in use should also be labeled. When releasing the lock on the lock rail, the rail operator should know what is hanging on that batten.

B.   Use Trim Marks

All rigging sets used during a performance should have trim marks on the hand lines. Tape, ribbon, yarn, or string can be used for this purpose (figure 4.44). If the piece must move quickly during the performance, winding the tape down the rope or inserting a warning yarn of a different color will indicate that the trim mark is approaching.

Ribbon trim marks can be pulled through the mantle of a parallel-core polyester line by using a crochet hook, tire repair tool, or a small screwdriver with a slot cut into the blade. Do not go through the center of the line (figure 4.45).

Pieces that do not move during a performance should also be marked, so that if they have to move for maintenance purposes, repositioning to performance trim is simplified.

4.44 Tape trim mark

4.45 Ribbon trim mark on parallel-core polyester line

C. Knuckle Buster

Accurate and fast positioning of a moving piece can be accomplished by using a knuckle buster on the hand line (figure 4.46). This clamp is designed to fit on the hand line without damaging the rope lock. However, in the dim light of a performance, a rail operator's knuckle or hand may be hit—hence the name.

4.46 Knuckle buster

D. Preshow Testing

Make a habit of running each moving piece before every performance. Test for balance, clearance, and ease of running. If the pull on the hand line feels different, find out why—before the performance!

Because soft goods absorb moisture from the air, the weight of a curtain or drop can change drastically with a change in humidity. Adjusting the counterweight on the arbor may be necessary on a daily basis in some theatres.

E. Cuing

Be absolutely sure of the signals for all cues during a performance.

A normal cue sequence consists of 3 parts, the 1-minute verbal warning, or cue, gives the operator time to find the proper hand line and determine what is supposed to happen. Does the piece move in or out? Are there special timing problems?

The next part is the standby cue, which occurs about 3 lines before the go cue and is often done by turning on a cue light. At this point, the rope lock is released and the operator is ready for the go.

Finally, the go cue is given. Because it is impossible for a person to watch 2 things at once, the operator generally watches the moving piece to be sure that there are no clearance problems.

If you feel any unusual resistance, stop moving the piece immediately. Chances are that it has fouled on another batten or flown object. The air currents in many theatres are different when the theatre is full (performance) and when the theatre is empty (rehearsal). Soft goods can blow and foul on adjacent objects. If you feel a problem, determine what it is before moving the piece. A powerful flashlight is a useful tool to have backstage for seeing into the dark flies.

4.14   Special Counterweight Rigging Problems

A.   Lighting Battens

Lighting battens frequently change weight as they are raised or lowered. This is caused by the border light cable, which is attached to the batten. In some rigging schemes, the cable is supported by a cradle attached to the lift lines. As the batten is raised, more weight is added to the batten. As the batten is lowered, weight is removed from the batten. In this circumstance, try to balance the batten for the performance trim height.

B.   Variable Load

Flying framed wall units with hinged side panels is one situation in which a change in load on the batten occurs. As the wall unit touches the floor and the hinged panels open, the floor—not the batten—is supporting the weight. The wall tends to bounce off the floor, leaving a gap at the bottom of the set. Here are 3 suggestions for dealing with this problem.

1. Block and Tackle

Use a block and tackle. Attach as described in section 4.12.B-4. As the flown piece touches the floor, the block and tackle is used to

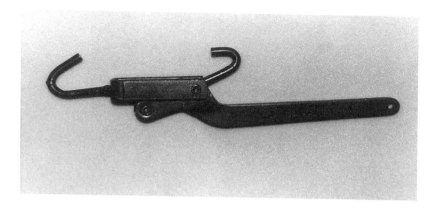

4.47 Load binder

raise the arbor and take the strain off the batten. This method requires 2 operators. One person operates the hand line, the other operates the lead line of the block and tackle.

2. Batten Tie-down

Attach wire or hemp ropes to the batten near the lift lines. As the flown piece nears the floor, the free ends of the ropes are tied off to brackets firmly attached to the stage floor or to a sandbag. Using a trucker's hitch for hemp, or a lever-type load binder for cable, usually gives the mechanical advantage needed to hold the batten in the desired position (figures 4.47 and 4.48).

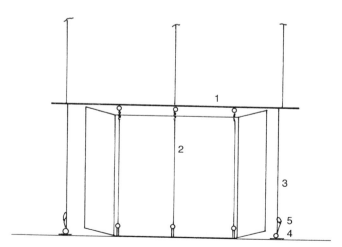

4.48 Batten tie-down
1. **Batten**
2. **Attachment line**
3. **Tie-down line**
4. **Ceiling plate**

3. Use a Carpet Hoist

See section 4.12.B-6.

C. Increasing the Counterweight Capacity

There may be times when an arbor will not hold enough counter-weight to balance a heavy load. *Do not use lead weights or an arbor extension without first checking the capacity of all components, including the support steel.* The line set was designed as a complete system, quite often with the arbor being the limiting factor in terms of applied weight. Using lead or an arbor extension may overload components beyond their working load limit. Suggested solutions to increase load capacity include:

1. Join two or more adjacent battens together, and use more than one line set. When doing this, be sure that the load is firmly attached to all of the battens and that the counterweight is evenly distributed among all the arbors. More than one operator may be required to move the battens. This solution distributes the load among the blocks and lift lines of several line sets and keeps all components within their working load limits.

2. After a careful analysis of the line set components (i.e., cable size, loft block, head block, support steel, attachment devices, etc.), to be certain they can sustain the added weight, you may substitute lead weights for steel weights. The density of lead is approximately 1.45 times that of steel.

3. Install a larger arbor or an arbor extension *after* analyzing the rest of the components to be sure that they can safely support the added load.

4. If there is room on the grid and in the flies, an additional free-hanging arbor may be used.

   a. Mount additional loft blocks over the batten. The blocks can be evenly spaced between the permanently mounted loft blocks or placed near the point of attachment of a concentrated load.

   b. A head block or a group of loft blocks is mounted on the grid in an area where the arbor has clear travel. Have the load capacity of the support steel checked to see if it can support the concentrated load of the loft and head blocks.

   c. Attach lift lines from the batten to the arbor.

   d. Since the arbor may not be near a loading bridge, a safe method of loading the arbor will have to be devised.

e. Arbor guide cables can be attached from the grid to the stage floor if necessary.

f. The area under the arbor must be roped off to keep people away during the performance.

CAUTION: In items 2 and 3 above, the flown object is solely supported by a single set of lift lines and blocks. IT IS ABSOLUTELY NECESSARY TO BE SURE THAT THE RIGGING SET AND SUPPORT STEEL CAN HOLD THE CONCENTRATED LOAD. Hire a structural engineer to make an analysis before attempting to increase the arbor load on any counterweight system.

4.15   Operation Summary

1. Safety inspect all components at regular intervals.
2. Know the feel, sound, and smell of the system.
3. Know the weight capacity of the system.
4. Always follow safe practice when loading, unloading, and operating the system. Keep unbalanced loads down.
5. Always appoint someone to maintain visual contact with a moving piece.
6. Be sure the deck is clear before moving a line set.
7. Always warn people on the stage and grid before moving a batten during set-in and load-out.
8. Before each cue, check the cue sheet to be sure which set is to move, which direction, and any special timing problems.

4.16   Safety-Inspection Summary

The following components should be inspected:

1. Hand lines
2. Arbor: (*a*) nuts on rods, (*b*) spreader bars and lock plates, (*c*) hand line knots, (*d*) casting and weld cracks, (*e*) guide system, (*f*) top and bottom blocks for a double-purchase set
3. Head and loft blocks: (*a*) mounting clamps, (*b*) support steel, (*c*) bearings, (*d*) fleet angle
4. Tension pulley: (*a*) travel, (*b*) bearings, (*c*) guides
5. Lock rail: (*a*) mounting bolts that hold the rail, (*b*) rope lock mounting bolts, (*c*) lock rings, (*d*) lock adjustment

6. Rope locks: (*a*) tension adjustment, (*b*) mounting bolts, (*c*) self-locking feature
7. Wire rope: (*a*) abrasion, (*b*) broken wires, (*c*) terminations at both ends
8. Battens: (*a*) splices, (*b*) level, (*c*) straight
9. Items not covered above

Part 5   Motorized Rigging

5.01   Introduction

The basic hemp rigging used for the stage changed little from the time of the Greeks until the 20th century. The need for greater efficiency prompted the modification of hemp to counterweight, which is still the most common type of rigging equipment in use. Today the desire for increased efficiency is fueling a greater use of motorized equipment.

Stage rigging manufacturers combine industrial-grade motors, speed reducers, brakes, controls, and special components to produce motorized rigging equipment for the entertainment industry. A motorized system must be properly designed for its application by a competent engineer. Because motorized rigging equipment is used to suspend objects over people, it requires operational safety devices not found on winches used in industry. Truck winches, industrial hoists, and boat winches are extremely dangerous to use in stage rigging, as are homemade systems, unmodified industrial systems, and Rube Goldberg equipment. DO NOT USE THEM.

A number of theatrical rigging equipment manufacturers now offer motorized equipment as standard products (figures 5.1 and

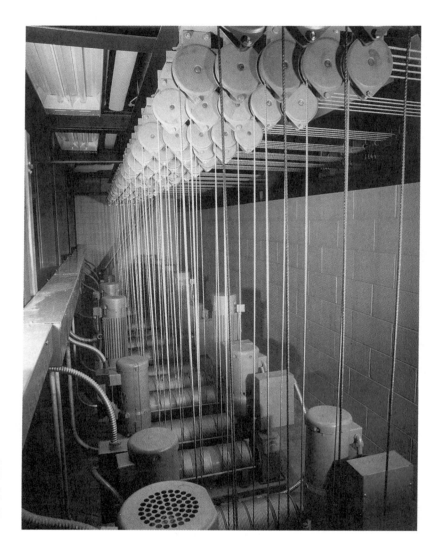

5.1 Electric motorized winches. Courtesy Peter Albrecht Corporation

5.2). Escalating labor costs and the equipment's versatility have helped hasten their acceptance. Broadway, touring productions, and regional professional companies use motorized equipment as a matter of course.

Some of the early motorized systems had design problems and lacked consistency of operation and dependability. As with any new technology, it took a while to refine and debug the systems. Since the 1960s, a great deal of motorized rigging has been installed throughout the world. The better systems are extremely reliable, ac-

5.2 Electric motorized winches. Courtesy Peter Albrecht Corporation

curate, and dependable. Motorized systems are the state of the art in rigging equipment today.

It is beyond the scope of this book to describe all of the types of systems in existence. I cover operating procedures for the most common types found in the United States.

The operator of motorized rigging does not have the physical contact with the moving object that is present when using hemp and counterweight systems. Therefore, you cannot feel when something changes or goes wrong. SPECIAL OPERATING PROCEDURES AND PRECAUTIONS FOR MOTORIZED RIGGING MUST BE FOLLOWED.

5.02   Systems Descriptions

The following descriptions are of general system types. Some of the advantages and problems are listed for each system.

A.   Motorized Counterweight Systems

A motorized counterweight system is basically a counterweight set that uses a motor to do the pulling. The motors do not need to be as large in horsepower as they would need to be in a straight (non-counterweight) motorized rigging system. One type requires counterweights to balance the load, so the same basic loading and un-

171

loading procedures used for a counterweight set should be followed. Another type of motorized counterweight system is designed to run out of balance, with the counterweight balancing only part of the load.

1. Chain-Drive, Wind-on–Wind-off Systems

The chain-drive system (figure 5.3) uses a roller chain attached to the arbor, much the same way that the hand line is attached to the arbor of a manual counterweight set. The chain goes from the top of the arbor, over a head block sprocket, down around a sprocket below the arbor, and finally to the underside of the arbor, where it attaches.

The winch is usually mounted on either the grid or below the stage-floor level. To reduce motor noise and to save space, it is preferable to mount the motor in a separate machine room. Some systems use a drive cable in place of a roller chain, but the basic operation principle is the same. One end of the cable is attached to the bottom of the arbor, the other end to the arbor top. One end of the cable winds on the drum as the other winds off (figure 5.4). Both of these systems are typically used for unbalanced applications, such as electric battens and lighting bridges.

2. Traction-Drive System

Traction-drive systems are generally used for constant-weight systems, such as acoustical reflectors, speaker clusters, large fire curtains, and movable ceiling panels (figures 5.5 and 5.6). Once the arbor is loaded and the weight balanced, the weight is never changed. In this system, the head block is usually machined with tight V-shaped grooves for the lift lines. The head block is driven by the motor and provides the force to move the load. As the head block turns, the V grooves grip the cable and move the load. Special care should be taken to inspect the cable and traction head blocks for wear.

B.   Straight Winch

The straight winch uses only the winch to move and hold the load (figure 5.7). This type of system usually requires a larger motor and gear reducer than does a motorized counterweight system. It is very efficient for rigging sets with changing loads. Set-up and take-down times are greatly reduced because no counterweights need to be loaded or unloaded.

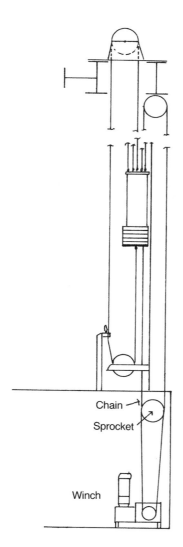

Chain

Sprocket

Winch

**5.3 Chain-drive
motorized
counterweight set**

C.   Line-Shaft System

A line-shaft system (figure 5.8) uses a grooved drum at each lift
line instead of running all of the lines back to a single drum. The
drums are connected to the motor and to each other by a common

**5.4 Wind-on–
wind-off winch**

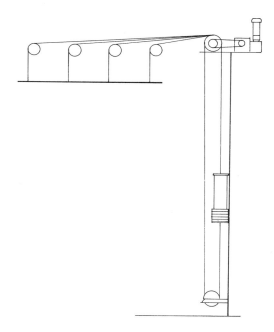

**5.5
Traction-drive
motorized
counterweight set**

**5.6
Traction-drive
fire curtain winch**

**5.7
Constant-speed
electric winch.
Courtesy Peter
Albrecht
Corporation**

5.8 Drum on line-shaft winch

shaft. If the lift lines drop straight down from each drum, there are no horizontal forces on the support steel.

5.03   Motor Types

There are 3 types of motors that are generally used for motorized rigging. Each has characteristics that make it more useful for some applications than others.

A.   AC Electric Motor

An AC motor is the least expensive and the easiest motor to use for single-speed applications. Variable-speed AC drives are available, but they are not as dependable for theatre use as DC drives.

B.   DC Electric Motor

A DC motor is reliable and dependable for variable-speed applications. It is also more expensive than an AC motor.

C.   Hydraulic Motor

Two types of rotary hydraulic motors are used for theatrical applications. The most common has an impeller blade mounted on a shaft that can either be a direct drive to the output shaft or be coupled to

5.9 Hydraulic motor on line-shaft winch

a speed reducer to increase the output torque (figure 5.9). Pressurized hydraulic fluid is forced through a valve, into an input port (making the impeller turn), then out through a return port. Reversing the direction of the fluid flow reverses the direction of the motor. The speed is controlled by operating the valve to regulate the flow of the hydraulic fluid.

A radial hydraulic motor is somewhat more complex, operating like a rotary aircraft engine. A number of pistons are mounted radially around the drive shaft. Fluid is forced sequentially into the cylinder heads, forcing the pistons toward the drive shaft. As the pistons move toward the shaft, they force the shaft to turn and produce rotary motion to turn a cable drum.

Another type—the linear hydraulic motor, or hydraulic ram—consists of a cylinder with a piston inside. Fluid is pumped through a valve on one side of the piston, forcing the piston to move along the length of the cylinder. The end of the piston is connected by a rod to the object that is to be moved. The most common use of the hydraulic ram is for stage and orchestra lifts, in which high speed and heavy load capacity are required. For rigging purposes, the end of the rod can be attached to a multisheave block, allowing a travel speed greater than the stroke of the piston (figure 5.10). With sufficient pressure, very high speeds can be attained with this type of system.

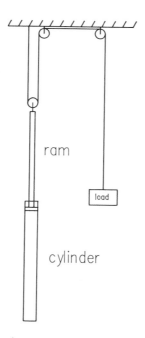

ram

cylinder

5.10 Hydraulic ram; load moves 2′ for every 1′ of ram movement

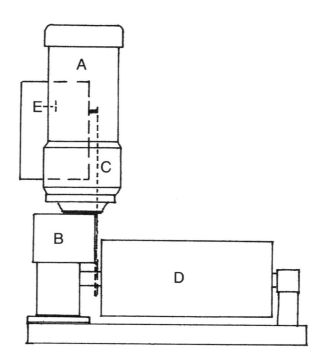

5.11 Electric winch components

5.04 Electric Winch Components

Electric winches usually consist of the following components (figure 5.11): (A) motor, (B) gear reducer, (C) brake, (D) drum, (E) controls.

A. Motor

The motor is the device that converts electrical energy into mechanical energy. The motor is either AC or DC.

B. Gear Reducer

The gear reducer converts a high number of revolutions with low torque into a lower number of revolutions with high torque (or lifting power). For many applications, self-locking gear reducers are preferred. These reducers require power to lower an object, as well as to raise it. The gear ratios are high enough so that the load cannot exert enough force on its own to move the gears, even if no motor brake is attached to the system. The self-locking feature should never be used alone. A properly sized brake is always required on a motorized rigging system.

Nonself-locking, or overhauling, gear reducers work conversely. These reducers are often used where very high efficiency is required or where the winches are self-climbing, such as in television studios. In this case, when the brake is released on the system, the load is capable of back-driving the gears, and the load descends without the motor running.

C. Brakes

Most electric winches use a motor brake, which is electrically held open when the winch is running. When the power is turned off, the brake closes and holds the load in place. The brake must be properly sized for the application. The load should stop moving from full speed in 6" or less.

Some winch systems employ a second brake system on the outboard end of the drum, serving as a backup brake. There are 2 types. One is similar to the motor brake. It is electrically held open when the winch is running and only sets when power to the machine is turned off. There have been some problems with this type of brake being synchronized to operate properly. The other type is an overspeed brake. It only kicks in if the winch starts to run past a preset speed. This type of secondary brake has proved to be much more dependable than the other.

D. Drum

On a straight electric winch, the lift lines wind on a grooved drum. The drum's grooves match the size of the cable being used. A minimum of 2 dead wraps of cable should be maintained on the drum.

Nongrooved pile-on drums, such as those found on hand winches, are sometimes used. As the wire rope winds on successive layers, the wire rope underneath is subjected to abrasion and crushing. Inspect the wire rope carefully, and replace it at the first sign of wear.

The yo-yo drum is another type of pile-on drum. It has a narrow groove that guides the wire rope to pile up on top of itself, just like a yo-yo. Because the radius from the wire rope to the center of the drum is constantly changing, the torque on the drum and speed of the wire rope are also constantly changing, thus making it a poor choice for variable-speed systems. Yo-yo drums are often found on self-climbing battens and motorized acoustic curtain systems. The main advantage of the yo-yo drum is that it eliminates any fleet angle problems.

E. Controls

Motorized rigging can be controlled in a number of different ways. Some of the typical components and methods are as follows:

1. Limit Switch

Most winches have a set of limit switches. These switches can be field adjusted for the maximum high and low trims. There should also be a set of overtravel switches, which serve as backups for the limit switches. Should the limit switch fail, the overtravel switch will stop the movement of the winch before damage can occur (figures 5.12 and 5.13).

2. Movement Controls

Movement controls can be categorized in 2 groups: hold-to-run (or deadman) and latching. The hold-to-run type requires constant hand pressure on the switch to keep the winch running. If pressure is removed, the winch stops. This type of control is the safest. Hold-to-run controls can be the push-button type or the joystick type. The push-button type is self-explanatory. A joystick is usually found on variable-speed systems. The farther the stick is pushed, the

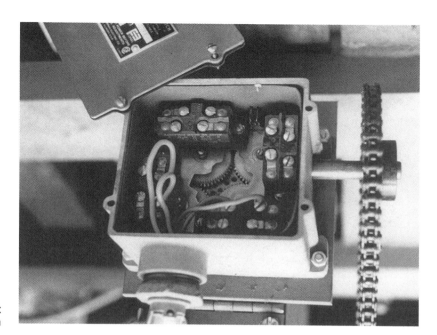

5.12 4-element rotary limit switch

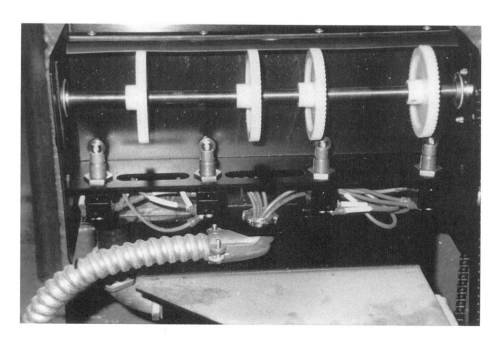

5.13 Traveling nut limit switch

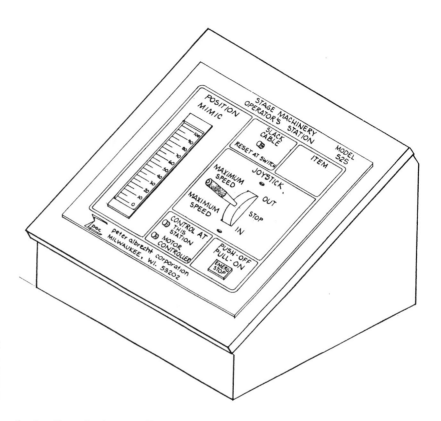

STAGE MACHINERY
OPERATOR'S STATION

POSITION
MIMIC

SLACK
CABLE

MODEL
525

RESET AT SWITCH

ITEM

MAXIMUM
SPEED

JOYSTICK

OUT

MAXIMUM
SPEED

STOP

IN

CONTROL AT
THIS
STATION

MOTOR
CONTROLLER

PUSH-OFF
PULL-ON

peter albrecht corporation
MILWAUKEE, WI. 53202

EMERG
STOP

**5.14 Joystick
winch control.
Courtesy Peter
Albrecht
Corporation**

faster the winch runs (figure 5.14). Pushing the stick in the opposite direction moves the winch in the opposite direction. The center
position stops winch movement and sets the brake.

Latching-type controls require only that the control be activated
to start the action. The control then is "latched in," and the winch
will run until a preset limit is reached. A separate control must be
activated to stop the winch, in case of an emergency. Latching controls require extra attention when the winch is operating because
the operator needs more time to stop the winch than with the hold-
to-run type: the operator must find the stop button and hit it. Using
the hold-to-run control, the operator merely releases pressure. It may
appear that a motorized rigging set runs very slowly, but when something fails and an object falls, it is extremely fast. It takes only about
2.5 seconds for something to fall from a 90'-high grid to the floor.

3. Emergency-Stop Button

All motorized winch systems should have an emergency-stop button (E-stop). The button should be large, easy to see, easy to

reach, and require pressure to activate. It should *not* require electrical power to operate. The E-stop should operate a contactor that removes power from all of the winches. On hydraulic systems, it should stop the pumps, thus removing power from the winches. An E-stop that only removes power from the control circuit is not reliable. Electronic control circuits can fail in such a way that the E-stop will not work. The E-stop is fail-safe only when it is on the power side of the system, not on the control side. On multiwinch systems, a single E-stop button should stop *all* of the machines.

4. Speed Controls

With variable-speed systems, you can select and adjust the speed of the winches. They must also have a tachometer to determine how fast the winch is turning. Some systems are designed to allow the synchronization of several machines. While this may be a desirable function, it is very costly.

5. Position Control

Many systems have some sort of device to allow for stopping the batten at a particular position. The important feature of positioning is repeatability. The load must stop at the same place when coming from the same direction every time. This feature is essential for the proper running of shows.

6. Other Safety Features

The *slack-cable switch* detects any slack cable on the winch set and stops the movement of the machine.

Load sensing measures the weight of the load on the batten through 2 or 3 cycles after the line set is loaded. It will then automatically stop the system if the load is increased or decreased beyond the programmed parameters.

Overspeed brakes keep the line set from running away. They sense if the winch drum is turning faster than a programmed speed and slow it down.

7. Computer Control

There are a number of different computer control consoles available for motorized rigging systems. Some of them use Programmable Logic Controller (PLC) technology, while others use specially designed software. All computerized systems require the winch components listed above, including limit switches, a tachometer, a position feedback device, and so on, as well as the computer.

For safe operation, there must be E-stop buttons located at strategic places. With computer controls, the operator has a wealth of information available on the monitor screens, but none of it is as critical as watching the moving object. If the operator cannot see the object that is moving, spotters must be used, and they must have the ability to communicate quickly with the operator or stop the object themselves in case of emergency.

F.   Rigging Components

The rigging components of motorized systems (the loft blocks, cables, battens, etc.) are the same as those used in counterweight rigging. The same care and precautions should be used on these components as on a counterweight system (see part 4).

5.05   Hydraulic Winch Components

Hydraulic power for the stage is transmitted by controlled circulation of pressurized fluid in a closed system. In addition to the required rigging components, a hydraulic system used for theatre work usually consists of the following components (figure 5.15):

1.   Electric power supply
2.   Hydraulic pump
3.   Hydraulic fluid feed line
4.   Hydraulic fluid return line
5.   Forward-reverse speed-control manifold
6.   Hydraulic motor
7.   Forward fluid line
8.   Reverse fluid line
9.   Control wiring to manifold
10.   Control panel
11.   Control wiring to pump

These systems are very efficient, but they require more maintenance than electric motors. Particular care should be given to filters, fluid, valves, and hoses.

5.06   Hand Winch

There are many different types of hand winches on the market. They are used for pulling boats onto trailers, raising basketball nets, and doing various other nontheatrical things. Most of them

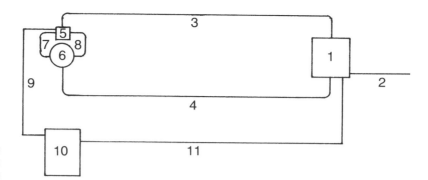

5.15 Hydraulic system components

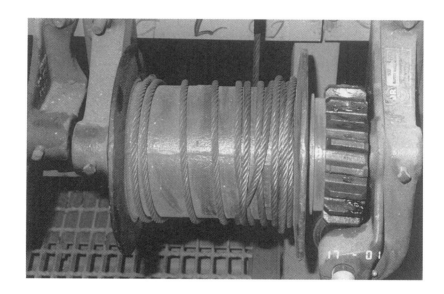

5.16 Hand winch with wire rope wound the wrong way

are not designed to hold objects safely over peoples' heads. Be sure that the hand winch that you are using is designed for both the load and the application for which you are using it.

Some hand winches are designed to be run with drill motors. Most are not. Running a hand winch with a motor produces operating speeds that are much faster than the gears were designed for. The gears will wear faster and eventually break, causing the load to fall. If the wire rope on your hand winch looks like figure 5.16, it is not wound on the drum in the correct direction. This leads to excessive crushing and reduces the life span of the wire rope. See figure 5.17 for the proper winding directions.

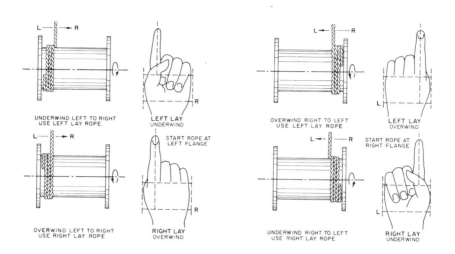

5.17 Winding wire rope on a smooth drum; by holding the right or left hand with index finger extended, palm up or palm down, the proper procedure for applying *left-* and *right-lay* rope on a smooth drum can easily be determined. Courtesy American Iron and Steel Institute, *Wire Rope Users Manual*

5.07   Operation of Motorized Rigging

A single person can operate many motorized rigging sets simultaneously. This is both an advantage and a danger. Because the operator does not have physical contact with the moving load through a hand line, it is imperative that visual contact with the moving load be maintained. If this is not possible, because of control location or because of the number of winches operating at one time, spotters—in audio contact with the winch operator—*must* be used.

It is absolutely necessary that the operator know the motorized equipment thoroughly. Answers to the following questions are essential before using any motorized system safely.

- What is the capacity of each winch?
- Are the gear reducers self-locking or overhauling?
- Are there overtravel switches on the limit switches?
- How do the controls work? (Hold-to-run? Latching?)
- How does the emergency-stop switch work? (Disconnect the power to the winches or only to the controls?)

186

A. Safety Inspect All Components

As with any rigging system, motorized rigging sets must be periodically inspected. In addition to inspecting the normal rigging components (see part 4), check the following:

1. Be sure the correct fuse size is installed.
2. Check all limit and overtravel switches.
3. Maintain oil in the gear reducer or hydraulic systems according to the manufacturer's instructions. Change the oil when necessary.
4. Test all controls for proper function.
5. Inspect winch mounting devices. They can pull loose!
6. Check the brake. If it chatters or the drum continues to turn after the winch is stopped, the brake may need adjustment.

B. System Capacity

It is essential to know the designed capacity of a motorized rigging set. Most are designed with the motor as the weakest part of the system. Any attempt to overload the system should result in the motor stalling out. However, not all systems are designed in this manner. Overloading the system can result in deflecting support steel or straining a component beyond its limit. FIND OUT THE CAPACITY OF THE SYSTEM; DISPLAY IT WHERE IT CAN BE SEEN; AND STAY WITHIN IT!

C. Loading and Unloading

1. Motorized Counterweight System

With a balanced-load motorized counterweight system, it is necessary to balance the load with weight on the arbor before operating the line set. As with a straight counterweight system, keep the weight down when loading or unloading. With this type of system, there is usually a clutch that will slip, or the motor will quickly overheat and cut out if the system is out of balance. Listening to the motor run in both directions can help you determine whether the system is balanced or not.

With a line set that is designed to run out of balance, the motor is the limiting factor. You should know the load capacity of the line set and the weight of the load that you place on it. If the line set is severely out of balance, a great deal of strain is placed on the drive chain or on the cable and motor. Overloading this type of system usually causes the motor to overheat, tripping the overload relay.

2. Straight Motorized System

Calculate the weight of the load before attaching it to the winch. If the machine stalls, if the overload relay trips, or if it sounds as if it is straining, it is overloaded. Do *not* use it in this condition.

D.   Showtime Operation

When the equipment is in safe operating condition, the operator thoroughly understands the controls, and all loads have been correctly attached, the motorized equipment is ready to be used during a performance.

If there are severe air currents backstage, or tight clearances that may cause problems, do a preshow check of any pieces that might foul. Either maintain visual contact with the moving pieces, or use a spotter. Read the cue sheets carefully! Be sure the right piece is moving on cue.

Listen carefully for any unusual sounds. Stop the moving piece immediately if a strange noise is heard.

Most motorized systems will stop much faster than a person can stop a counterweight system. This is a safety advantage in case of fouling.

5.08   Operation Summary

1. Know the system.
2. Safety inspect all components at regular intervals.
3. Always follow safe practice when loading and unloading.
4. Be sure that everyone and everything are clear before moving a piece.
5. Maintain visual contact or use a spotter.
6. Always warn people onstage and on the grid before activating a winch during set-in or strike.
7. Before each cue, check your cue sheet to see which piece to move, which direction, and any special problems.

5.09   Safety-Inspection Summary

1. All rigging components (see part 4)
2. All lubricated parts on the winches: (*a*) gearbox, (*b*) pillow blocks, (*c*) motor bearings

3. Hydraulic connections, fluid level, filters
4. Limit and overtravel switches
5. Control system
6. Brakes
7. Emergency-stop control

Part 6 Cutting and Knotting Rope, Attaching Loads, Special Problems

6.01 Fiber Rope

Fiber rope is made of natural or synthetic fibers that are either twisted or braided into yarns and then into rope.

A. Cutting

There are specific procedures for cutting different kinds of rope.

1. Natural Fiber

Twisted natural-fiber rope should be taped with electrician's friction tape before cutting. This tape is easy to remove and will keep the ends from fraying. Tape about a 2" length of rope where the cut is to be made. Use a pair of garden pruning shears and cut the rope in the center of the tape (figure 6.1). After the rope is cut, remove the tape and whip the end, using small twine (figure 6.2).

6.1 Cutting fiber rope

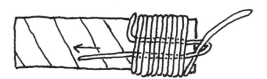

6.2 Whipping hemp

Braided natural fiber, such as cotton sash cord, need not be taped for cutting; pruning shears work best for the job. If the rope is to be used for a long time, whipping, dipping the ends in glue, or taping will keep the ends neat. Braided rope is not as susceptible to fraying as twisted rope.

2. Synthetic Fiber

Synthetic-fiber rope is best cut with a heated knife designed for this purpose. Live flame can be substituted, if the knife is unavailable. Hold the rope in both hands and rotate it over a flame. Gently pull it apart as you rotate it. The ends can be shaped before they completely cool by pushing them against a hard surface. This method not only cuts the rope but binds the fiber ends together to prevent unraveling (figure 6.3).

6.3 Cutting nylon rope

B. Knots

A knot is used to attach a rope to an object. Knots reduce the breaking strength of rope and can slip or come untied if misapplied. Therefore, the proper knot for a specific application must be used. Knot *efficiency* is the remaining strength of a rope after a knot has been tied in it. The following is a list of the efficiencies of common stage knots. These are average values and will vary depending on a number of conditions.

Knot	Efficiency
Bowline	60%
Figure-8	64%
Two half hitches	
around a 15-mm-dia. ring	60%
around a 96-mm-dia. post	65%
Square knot	43%
Clove hitch	75%
Clove hitch with 2 half hitches	65%
Eye splice with thimble	95%

1. Bowline

Use a bowline (figure 6.4) when tying a loop in the end of a rope.

2. Clove Hitch

A clove hitch is used for tying a rope to a rigid object, such as a batten. When properly tied, it does not slip sideways (figure 6.5).

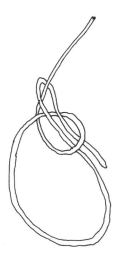

6.4 Bowline

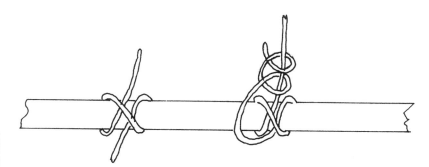

6.5 Clove hitch with 2 half hitches

3. Stopper Hitch

A stopper hitch (figure 6.6) is used to tie the safety rope onto a counterweight hand line. (See section 4.11.A-2.)

4. Prusik

Another knot used to tie a safety line on a counterweight hand line is a prusik. It can also be used to attach a rope sunday to a hand line for use with a block and tackle (figure 6.7).

5. Half Hitch

The half hitch (figure 6.8) can be used to secure the counterweight safety rope to the lock rail.

6.6 Stopper hitch

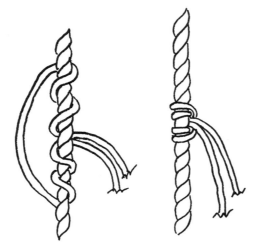

6.7 Prusik knot

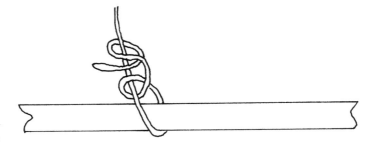

6.8 2 half hitches

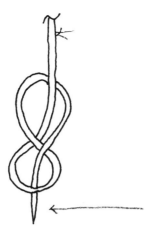

6.9 Figure-8 knot

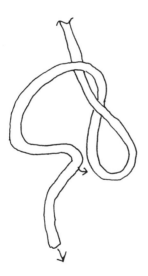

6.10 Trucker's
hitch

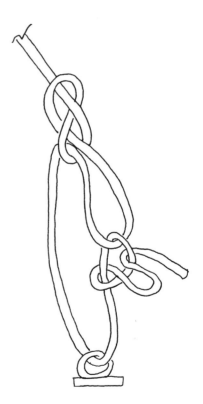

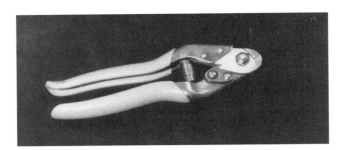

6.11 Small wire-rope cutter

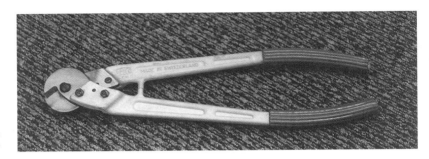

6.12 Large wire-rope cutter

6. Figure-8 Knot

The figure-8 knot (figure 6.9) is used at the end of a spot line to hold a length of pipe as a weight. (See section 3.08.F.)

7. Trucker's Hitch

The trucker's hitch (figure 6.10) is used when flying framed scenery with hemp or when tying a batten down to a floor hold. (See section 4.14.B-2.)

6.02   Wire Rope

Cutting, handling, and terminating wire rope all require special care. Carelessness can result in damage and loss of strength to the wire rope.

A.   Cutting

There are several different kinds of wire-rope cutters available on the market. For sizes up through 1/8", small handheld cutters can be used (figure 6.11). For larger sizes, 2 hand cutters or a cold chisel must be used (figure 6.12).

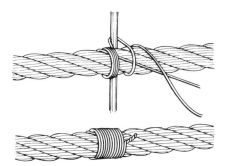

NEVER try to use a standard pair of wire cutters! Not only will they do a poor job but they will be ruined in the process.

Tape the wire rope before cutting. If the wire rope is to have a free end, *seizing* is required. Seizing is whipping the end with thin wire (figure 6.13).

B. Unreeling and Uncoiling

Great care should be taken when unreeling or uncoiling wire rope. Carelessness can cause kinking. A kink can never be removed and must be cut out. When taking wire rope from a reel, place the reel on an axle so that it can rotate. Grasp the wire rope and walk away from the reel. Take care that the reel does not turn too fast and dump wire rope in a pile on the ground.

If the reel is too large to be supported by an axle, let the end of the wire rope rest on the floor, and roll the reel away from the end.

Coiled lengths of wire rope must be handled very carefully. Unroll the coil in your hand as you walk along, or roll it along the floor. DO NOT UNCOIL BY PULLING ONE END.

C. Terminating

Terminating (attaching the end of a wire rope to an object) must be done carefully. It is important to maintain maximum wire-rope strength. It is also necessary to be sure that the termination will not slip.

A thimble is always used when forming a loop in the end of a wire rope. The rope is fastened using either wire-rope clips or compression sleeves.

1. Wire-Rope Clips

Wire-rope clips are manufactured from 2 types of material: cast

6.14 Malleable clip saddle on left, forged on right

6.15 2 malleable saddles; note differences in size and quality

malleable iron and forged steel (figure 6.14). For load-bearing applications, use only forged clips.

The saddles for malleable clips are cast, and the casting quality varies widely (figure 6.15). The casting process can also produce hidden voids causing a weakness in the cast part that is not visible to the naked eye. The hidden voids usually cause failure when the clip is being tightened or, more seriously, under shock load. Only one U.S. company manufactures malleable clips domestically and puts its name on the product. All other malleable clips are manufactured offshore and have only the country of origin stamped on them, making it impossible to trace or obtain application information about them.

Malleable clips are *not* rated for load-bearing applications and should not be used for rigging. They are designed for nonload-bearing uses, such as guy wires.

Forged clips are designed to be used for load-bearing applications. Hot steel is beaten into shape by forging dies to form the saddle, eliminating any chance of hidden voids. The U-bolt and nuts are larger than those used for the malleable clips.

The number of clips, the spacing of the clips, and the proper tightening of the clips are necessary to make a correct termination.

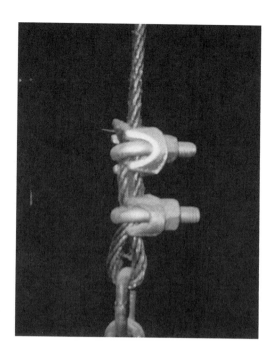

6.16 Clips installed too close together

If you use the correct number of clips and the proper tightening torque, you reduce the tendency for the clips to slip under load. The proper spacing on the clips is necessary to keep the clips from slipping if the top clip is pulled up into a sheave or against some other object. When pulled against an object, the top clip tends to slip along the live line, and the dead end tends to bend out and pook away from the live line. The resulting kink helps keep the dead end of the line from pulling out of the clips (figure 6.16).

There are 2 types of forged wire-rope clips commonly used for stage rigging: U-bolt and fist grip. The efficiency of both types is the same.

When using U-bolt clips, extreme care must be exercised to make certain that they are attached correctly; that is, the U-bolt must be applied so that the U section is in contact with the dead end of the rope and the saddle on the live end. REMEMBER, NEVER SADDLE A DEAD HORSE. Also, the tightening and retightening of the nuts must be accomplished as required.

How to apply clips. Recommended method of applying U-bolt clips (figure 6.17) to get maximum holding power of the clip (figures 6.18 and 6.19):

1. Turn back the specified amount of rope from the thimble. Ap-

6.17 Forged U-bolt wire-rope clip. Courtesy American Iron and Steel Institute, *Wire Rope Users Manual*

6.18 Correct order of installing clips. Courtesy Columbus McKinnon Corporation

ply the first clip one base width from the dead end of the wire rope (U-bolt over dead end; live end rests in clip saddle). Tighten the nuts evenly.

2. Apply the next clip as near to the loop as possible. Turn nuts firmly, but do not tighten.

3. Space additional clips, if required, equally between the first 2. Turn nuts; take up rope slack; and tighten all nuts evenly on all clips to recommended torque.

4. NOTICE: *Apply the initial load and retighten nuts to the recommended torque. Rope will stretch and be reduced in diameter when loads are applied. Inspect periodically and retighten to recommended torque.*

A termination made in accordance with the above instructions and using the number of clips shown has an approximate 80% efficiency rating. This rating is based on the catalog breaking strength of wire rope. If a pulley is used in place of a thimble for turning back the rope, add one additional clip.

The number of clips shown is based on using right regular-lay or

U-Bolt

Clip Size (in)	Min. No. of Clips	Amount of Rope to Turn Back (in)	Torque lb/ft
1/8	2	3¼	4.5
3/16	2	3¾	7.5
¼	2	4¾	15.0
5/16	2	5¼	30.0
3/8	2	6½	45.0
7/16	2	7	65.0
½	3	11½	65.0

From the Crosby Group

lang-lay wire rope, 6 X 19 class or 6 X 37 class, fiber-core or IWRC, IPS or XIPS. If Seale construction or similar large outer-wire-type construction in the 6 X 19 class is used for sizes 1" and larger, add one additional clip. The number of clips shown also applies to right regular-lay wire rope, 8 X 19 class, fiber-core, IPS, sizes 1½" and smaller; and right regular-lay wire rope, 18 X 7 class, fiber-core, IPS or XIPS, sizes 1¾" and smaller.

For other classes of wire rope not mentioned above, it may be necessary to add additional clips to the number shown.

If a greater number of clips are used than shown in the table, the

Right Way for Maximum Rope Strength

Wrong Way: Clips Staggered

Wrong Way: Clips Reversed

6.19 Clip application. Courtesy American Iron and Steel Institute, *Wire Rope Users Manual*

Fist-Grip Clip

Clip Size (in)	Min.No. of Clips	Amount of Rope to Turn Back (in)	Torque (lb/ft)
3/16–1/4	2	4	30
5/16	2	5	30
3/8	2	5½	45
7/16	2	5½	65
1/2	3	11	65

From the Crosby Group

6.20 Forged fist-grip wire-rope clip. Courtesy American Iron and Steel Institute, *Wire Rope Users Manual*

amount of rope turn-back should be increased proportionately. THE ABOVE IS BASED ON THE USE OF CLIPS ON NEW ROPE.

IMPORTANT: Failure to make a termination in accordance with the aforementioned instructions, or failure to periodically check and retighten to the recommended torque, will cause a reduction in efficiency rating.

How to apply fist-grip clips. Recommended method of applying fist-grip clips (figure 6.20):

1. Turn back the specified amount of rope from the thimble. Apply the first clip one base width from the dead end of the wire rope. Tighten nuts evenly to recommended torque.

2. Apply the next clip as near to the loop as possible. Turn nuts firmly, but do not tighten.

3. Space additional clips, if required, equally between the first 2. Turn the nuts; take up rope slack; tighten all nuts evenly on all clips to recommended torque.

4. NOTICE: *Apply the initial load and retighten the nuts to the recommended torque. The rope will stretch and be reduced in diameter when loads are applied. Inspect periodically and retighten to recommended torque.*

A termination made in accordance with the above instructions and using the number of clips shown has, approximately, an 80% efficiency rating. This rating is based on the catalog breaking strength of wire rope. If a pulley is used in place of a thimble for turning back the rope, add one additional clip.

The number of clips shown is based on using right regular-lay or lang-lay wire rope, 6 X 19 or 6 X 37 class, fiber-core or IWRC, IPS or XIPS. If Seale construction or similar large outer-wire-type construction in the 6 X 19 class is to be used for sizes 1" and larger, add one additional clip.

The number of clips shown also applies to right regular-lay wire rope, 8 X 19 class, fiber-core, IPS, sizes 1½" and smaller; and right regular-lay wire rope, 18 X 7 class, fiber-core, IPS or XIPS, sizes 1½" and smaller.

For other classes of wire rope not mentioned above, it may be necessary to add additional clips to the number shown.

If a greater number of clips are used than shown in the table, the amount of rope turn-back should be increased proportionately. THE ABOVE IS BASED ON THE USE OF FIST-GRIP CLIPS ON NEW WIRE ROPE.

IMPORTANT: Failure to make a termination in accordance with the aforementioned instructions, or failure to periodically check and retighten to the recommended torque, will cause a reduction in efficiency rating.

Fist-grip clips do not damage the wire rope the way U-bolt clips do. For this reason, they are preferred for temporary uses, such as hanging scenery.

2. Compression Sleeves

When properly applied, copper compression sleeves (also called Nicopress sleeves) provide a termination with 100% efficiency (figure 6.21). Carefully follow the manufacturer's instructions.

Figures 6.22 through 6.25 illustrate the proper way to apply a sleeve to ³⁄₁₆" aircraft wire rope. The order of making the crimps is not important.

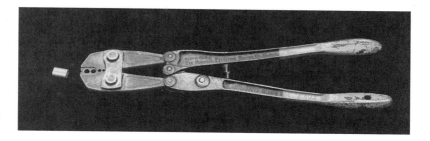

6.21 Nicopress crimping tool

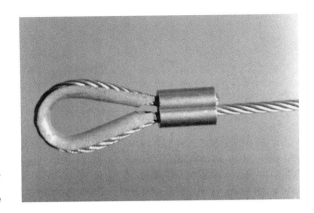

6.22 Nicopress sleeve on 3/16" aircraft cable

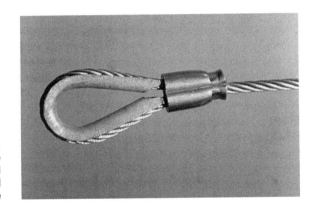

6.23 First crimp; end of cable should extend out from end of sleeve

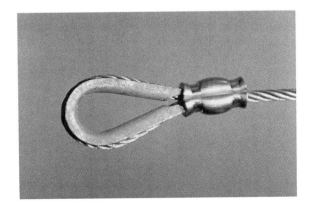

6.24 Second crimp

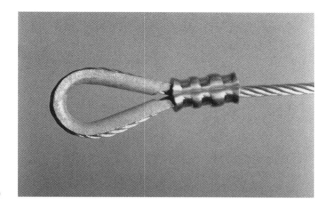

6.25 Third crimp

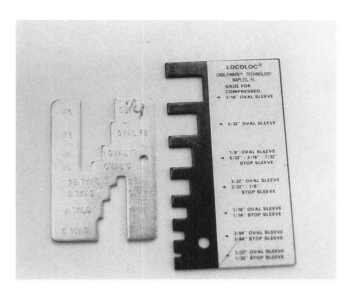

6.26 Go gauges from 2 different manufacturers

To make a proper termination:

a. Use the right size copper sleeve.
b. The wire rope must extend all the way through the sleeve.
c. The sleeve should not deform against the thimble.
d. The crimping tool must be properly calibrated.
e. Use the correct number of compressions.
f. Align the sleeve with about ⅛" of wire rope protruding from the top of the sleeve.
g. Make the first crimp.

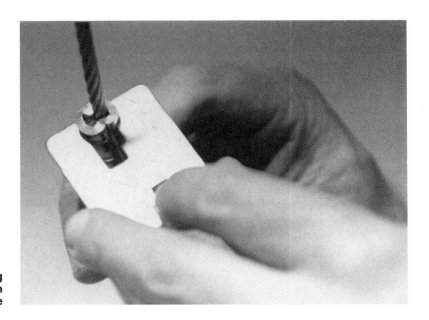

h. Make the second crimp.

i. Make the third crimp.

j. Check the crimps with manufacturer's go–no-go gauge (figures 6.26 and 6.27). If necessary, adjust the tool and crimp again. The tool should be checked after every 50 crimps.

3. Trim Chains

Trim chains are used in many ways to attach loads to battens. A typical scenery trim chain consists of a welded or forged steel ring, a length of chain, and a device to attach the chain to itself (usually a snap hook). One should take care to find out the safe working load of a trim chain before using it.

Manufacturers' catalogs usually give that information for the chain and the ring. It is almost impossible to find a rating for snap hooks. Because snap hooks are unrated, they should not be used for any heavy load. Many theatres are replacing the snap hooks with shackles. The chain can be attached to the batten either by sliding the ring on the batten between the lift lines, passing the chain around the batten and through the ring, or by wrapping the chain around the batten 1½ times and attaching it to itself (figure 6.28).

If the strength of the trim chain is in doubt, do not use it, or use

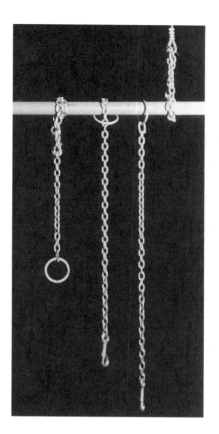

**6.28 Trim chains
 on a batten**

more chain to distribute the load. If the strength of the snap hook is in doubt, use a shackle.

6.03   Bolts

A great deal of rigging hardware is clamped together by bolts. One of the primary examples of this is clamping head and loft blocks to the support steel; and an examination of any rigging system will reveal many other examples of bolts clamping components together. In a clamping application, as the nut is tightened, the bolt is put in tension and actually stretches. The nuts are made of a slightly softer material than the bolts. There is a tolerance between the threads of the nut and the threads of the bolt. You can feel the slop by wiggling a new nut on a new bolt. As the nut tightens, the threads of the nut deform and become fully engaged with the threads on the bolt. This maximum contact allows enough force to stretch the bolt. Once the threads in a nut have been deformed, they are never as strong again because they have been stretched past their yield point. If you are "kicking sheaves" or have to disassemble a component that has been clamped together, it is a good idea to replace the nuts. The bolt manufacturers purposely make the nut the softer material because it is easier and cheaper to replace than the bolt.

Bolts are tightened with torsional force, which is far more destructive than the compression force on the pieces of metal that they are clamping together. If the bolt and the metal pieces being clamped are the same strength material, it is fairly easy to strip the bolt or wring the head off. There are 3 major grades of bolts readily available, and using the right grade for a specific application is essential for having a safe rigging system. The grade is based on the ultimate breaking strength of the material from which the bolt and nut are made. *The nut and bolt must be the same grade.* If you mix the grades, the weakest component will easily strip and you will not be able to get the proper tension in the bolt.

Figure 6.29 shows the markings for the 3 grades of nuts and bolts. Grade 2 bolts are the common variety found in local hardware stores. These are fine for clamping legs on platforms or any wood-to-metal application. *Grade 5 bolts should be used for almost all rigging components.* Grade 8 bolts are used for clamping high-strength steel together and other special applications.

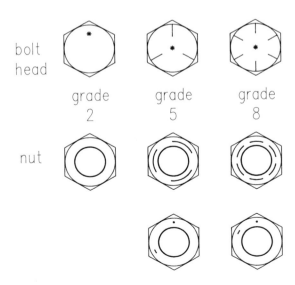

6.29 Nut and bolt grade marks (* manufacturer's identification mark)

6.04   Attaching Loads

A.   Curtains

Curtains are attached to battens by using tie lines. Some of the standard procedures for tying curtains follow.

1. Knots

Always use bow knots. This knot will securely hold the load, and untying the curtain will be easy.

2. Full Stage-Width Curtains

On full stage-width curtains, start tying in the center of the batten.

3. Excess Curtain Width

Fold excess curtain back on the offstage side.

4. Overlap Panels

Overlap the panels by at least one tie line. Overlapping by 2 will ensure a less-obvious break in the panels.

5. Tied-in Fullness

When tying fullness into a flat-sewn curtain, tie the ends first (figure 6.30). Then tie the center tie to a center point on the batten between the 2 end ties. Continue tying the center ties of the remaining sections of curtain to the centers of the remaining spaces. This will produce even fullness in the goods.

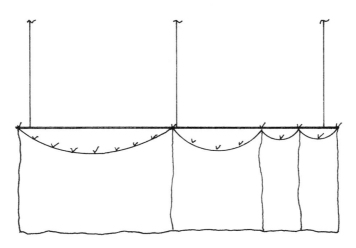

6.30 Tying fullness in a curtain

6. Soft Edge Legs

For a softer look on the onstage edge of the legs, fold the sewn edge back one or more ties.

7. Bent Batten

If the legs on the batten are very heavy and bend the batten, apply weight to the center of the batten: sandbags or a length of pipe can be tied, chained, or clamped to the batten.

B. Drops

If drops are not made with grommets and ties, sandwich battens must be used along the top edge.

1. Grommets and Ties

Tie a drop to a batten the same way that a full stage-width curtain is tied. Start at the center point, and work toward the offstage ends.

2. Sandwich Batten

The top of a drop can be sandwiched between 2 pieces of 1" X 3" pine that are screwed together. The drop is pierced just below the sandwich batten near the ends and about every 10'. Trim chains can then be used to attach the drop to the pipe batten.

The chains are attached to the pipe batten by passing the free end around the batten and through the ring. The chains are pulled snug to the pipe batten. The free end is then passed through the drop and attached back on the chain. This method allows easy leveling of crooked drops.

An alternate method is to drill ½" holes through the sandwich batten and use no. 8 sash cord to tie the drop to the pipe batten.

3. Pipe Weight

A common method of adding weight to a drop is to sew a pocket into the bottom and insert a length of ½" pipe as a weight. Be sure the ends of the pipe are secured to the drop to prevent the pipe from slipping out if one end of the drop should foul.

4. Pipe Weight Safety

Use small-diameter wire ropes for safety if the drop requires a pipe larger than ½" and if it is so close to another object that there is danger of the pipe pocket tearing and the pipe falling out.

Attach ¹/₁₆" or ⅛" wire rope to the pipe batten every 10' or 12' and near the ends of the drop. Let the wire ropes hang down on the back side of the drop. Pierce the pipe pocket on the back side, then secure the other end of the wire ropes to the batten weight pipe, using a clove hitch and wire-rope clip. Even if the drop tears completely away, the added wire ropes will hold the weight pipe. SAFETY CABLES ARE A MUST FOR ALL DROPS USED IN A'VISTA CHANGES. Wire rope of 1/16" will usually be strong enough and, if painted black, will not be noticeable even through a scrim.

C. Vertical Framed Scenery

Vertical framed scenery is anything that has a rigid frame and hangs in a vertical plane.

1. Hardware Attachment

Put at least one bolt through every piece of hardware on a flying unit. This is especially important on all hanger irons used to attach the unit to fly lines.

2. Calculate Load

The load will probably not be evenly distributed to all support lines (see figure 3.17). Be sure the support lines have a minimum design factor of 5:1. If people must move under the load while it is moving, increase the design factor to 10:1.

3. Point of Attachment

Traditionally the point of attachment for hard-framed scenery has been at the bottom for 2 reasons. First, it is easier to level the unit if the adjustment devices are at the bottom. Second, by attaching at the bottom, the framing members are in compression instead of tension. With wooden flats held together with nails and corrugated fasteners, having the joints in compression provides added strength to the joints. The disadvantage of attaching the support lines at the bottom is that the scenic unit tends to tilt and not hang plumb.

   Placing the point of attachment at the top requires using a ladder to level the unit. It also places the framing members in tension and adds stress to the joints. With proper design of the framing members and joints, issues of strength can be resolved. The advantage of top attachment is that the unit generally will not tilt.

4. Attaching with Rope

Rope is used when the weight of the unit is within the load limits of rope and when the attaching lines will not be visible (figure 6.31). Tie the rope to the batten with a clove hitch and 2 half hitches.

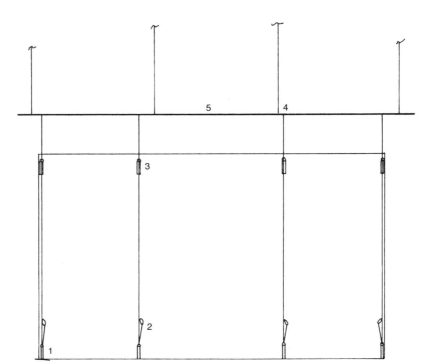

6.31 Framed scenery attached to batten with fiber rope

1. **Bottom hanger iron**
2. **Trucker's hitch**
3. **Top hanger iron**
4. **Clove hitch**

6.32 Top hanger iron

Pass the rope through the top hanger irons (figure 6.32). Attach it to the bottom hanger irons (figure 6.33) using a trucker's hitch. The hitch will allow easy adjustment for leveling the unit. If the unit is properly designed, the hitch can be applied to the top hanging hardware.

6.33 Bottom hanger iron

6.34 Boat or line eye

5. Attaching with Wire Rope

Attach the wire rope to the batten by wrapping it around the batten with a clove hitch and fastening the end with clips. An alternate method is to make a loop around a thimble, using wire-rope clips or compression sleeves. This loop is then attached to a trim chain on the batten. The wire rope is then run through a boat eye (figure 6.34) and attached to a jaw-eye turnbuckle.

The jaw end is attached to the bottom hanger iron. Leveling of the piece can then be easily accomplished from the bottom (figure 6.35). The wire rope can also be attached to a properly designed top hanger. For attaching at the top, the turnbuckle can be either at the scenery or at the batten end of the wire rope.

D. Horizontal Framed Scenery

Horizontal framed scenery units (figure 6.36), such as ceilings, hang parallel to the stage floor. It is important to have enough pickup points to distribute the load on the frame. Ceiling plates (figure 6.37) bolted to the frame are used to attach pickup lines of either hemp or wire rope.

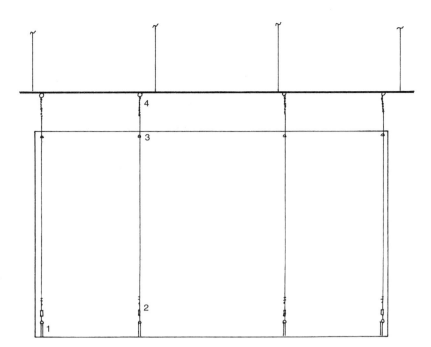

6.35 Framed scenic unit hung with wire rope
1. Bottom hanger iron
2. Turnbuckle
3. Boat eye

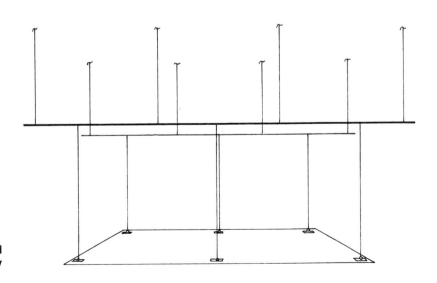

6.36 Horizontal framed scenery

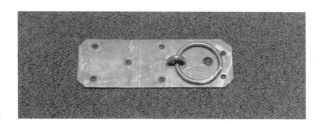

6.37 Ceiling plate

E. Point Loads

A *point load* is the load on a single support point (figure 6.38). The point must be capable of supporting the load imposed on it. When attaching a load to a batten, it is best to keep the attachment points as close to the lift lines as possible. This will keep the batten from bending and lift line wire ropes from becoming slack (figure 6.39).

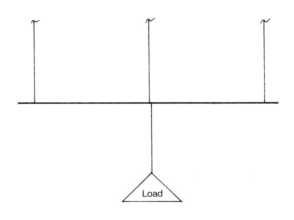

6.38 Point load on a batten

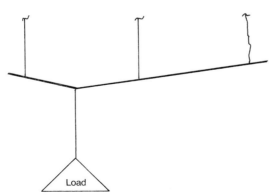

6.39 Point load bending a batten

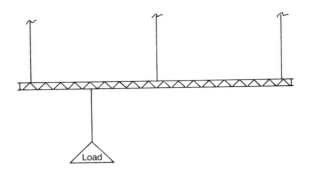

**6.40 Point load
on a truss batten**

1. Truss Batten

One method of distributing the load more evenly is to use a *truss batten* (figure 6.40). The truss is made of 2 battens (spaced from several inches to a foot apart) with welded or bolted support members. If the truss is overloaded, the top member will tend to buckle and bend outward. A box or triangular truss is more resistant to buckling and can generally hold heavier loads than 2-dimensional trusses.

2. Bridling

Bridling is another way to distribute the load (figure 6.41). The same technique can be used to distribute dead-hung loads attached to the grid (figure 6.42). See section 1.05 for calculating load information on bridles.

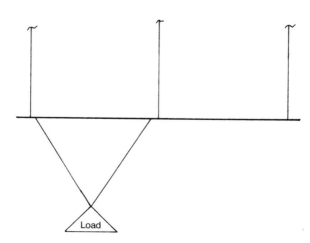

**6.41 Load on a
bridle**

6.05   Special Problems

A.   Breasting

There are times when it is necessary to move a flown piece in a horizontal, as well as a vertical, direction. This can be done by breasting the piece (figure 6.43). Breasting is a form of bridling and the loading must be calculated accordingly.

B.   Tripping

Tripping is a method of flying a very high drop when the grid is too

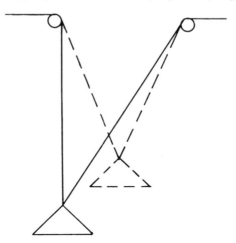

6.43 Breasting

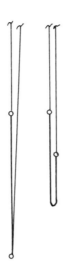

6.44 Tripping

low (figure 6.44). An additional set of lift lines is attached to the weight pipe in the bottom of the drop. As the trip lines are raised, the load on the main flying set is reduced. The hand line of the main flying set should be tied off with a safety hitch before raising the trip lines.

C. Guiding

In very close quarters, a drop or piece of scenery may require guide cables to keep it from fouling (figure 6.45). If guide cables are not possible, lengths of rope, called tag lines, can be attached to the end of the batten or an adjacent batten (figure 6.46). As the piece is moving in or out, crew members guide it with the tailing ropes.

D. Dead Hanging

Units may be dead hung from the grid. When necessary, distribute the load to more than one grid member (figure 6.47). If bridling is not possible, pass the support line through the grid and attach it to a piece of steel or wood that has been laid on the grid. This will help to distribute the load.

E. Flying People

Flying people in the entertainment industry is a very special skill. If the goal of flying people is just to lift them up in the air, then moun-

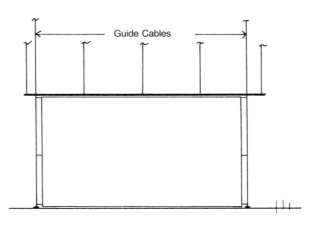

6.45 Guide lines on a drop

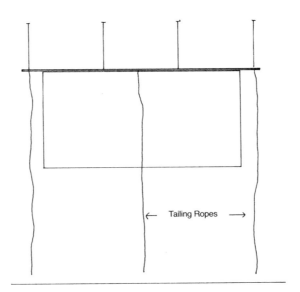

6.46 Tag lines on a batten

tain-climbing, rescue, or fall-protection techniques can be used. Contact experts in those fields for assistance. But if the goal is to create magic and give the illusion that a person is flying through space with no visible means of support, then the services, expertise, and special equipment of a company specializing in flying people are required.

The rigging equipment used for these special effects is not for sale from theatrical supply houses. Much of it is designed and manufactured by these specialized companies. The equipment is

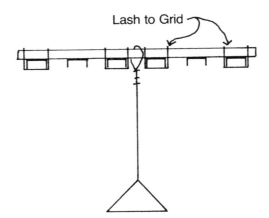

Lash to Grid

6.47 Distributing a dead-hung load on a grid

designed to be used under very strict supervision. It is rigorously tested before installation and meticulously inspected before every performance. Because of the high degree of risk involved with flying people, only professionally manufactured equipment installed under the supervision of an experienced flying technician should be used.

Never use homemade equipment for flying people. Standard heavy-duty traveler-track hardware, blocks, and other components will not stand up to the complex dynamic forces of flying a person. A number of former Peter Pans and ex-Santa Clauses still suffer from injuries they sustained while being flown on homemade equipment.

6.06   Recordkeeping

One of the questions asked after an accident is whether the rigging equipment has been inspected and properly maintained on a regular basis. *Rigging equipment is machinery. It requires care and maintenance.* Because it suspends objects over the heads of people, it poses a high degree of risk to life and limb. Failure to care for rigging equipment is negligent behavior. Performing regular inspections and correcting problems as they occur and before they are serious are required procedures in order to ensure the safety of everyone working on the stage or under any suspended object.

Two sets of records are of great value in maintaining and ensuring the safety of rigging equipment. They are (1) a rail log and (2) an inspection and maintenance log. By keeping written records you do not have to rely on anyone's memory, and you have written documentation of the care and diligence used in the facility in case of an accident. The written records can be an important tool in risk management, and they could hold critical information if there is a change of personnel.

A.   Rail Log

Rigging components wear out due to stress and fatigue. It is much easier to predict when failure will occur if a record is kept of the use of each line set. Develop a simple form that is filled out for each production that comes into the facility. The form should include the following:

1.   The name of the production
2.   The dates of the run
3.   A listing of each line set
4.   The amount of weight on the line set
5.   The number of times the line set moves during each performance

The format can be modified to fit the type of use for your particular venue. The important items are the weight per line set and the amount of use, determined by the number of cycles during a given period. More heavily used line sets will require more frequent inspection and component replacement.

B.   Inspection and Maintenance Log

Develop a written log to record the periodic inspections and maintenance of the equipment. The basic items that the log should include are as follows:

1.   The date of inspection
2.   The name of the inspector
3.   Check sheets that contain space for each component of each line set inspected
4.   What items required repair or replacement
5.   When the repair or replacement work was done
6.   The name of the person doing the repair or replacement

6.07   Operator Training

The third principle—*know how to use the system*—can only happen with proper training. Since every rigging system is unique, *all operators in a given facility should be trained to use that specific system.* The training should be systematic and complete. The way to accomplish this is to develop a comprehensive training program for each individual facility. The training program should include:

1. Checklist of specific skills to be taught
2. Instruction in each item on the list
3. Adequate opportunity to practice and develop the skill required for each item
4. Competency testing of each skill on the checklist
5. Awarding a certificate of competency upon successful completion of the test

The checklist of specific skills should include:

1. Loading and unloading procedures
2. Working the rail and loading bridge (or bridges)
3. Attaching loads to battens
4. All methods of safety tie-offs used
5. Setting up and operating a bull line (also a bull winch and capstan winch, if available)
6. All hemp-rigging procedures used in this particular facility
7. Operation and maintenance of all motorized equipment
8. Knot tying
9. Inspecting the system
10. Maintaining the inspection and maintenance log
11. Maintaining the rail log
12. Any special equipment or procedures necessary and peculiar to this facility

A part of any rigging competency training program should include training in developing good work habits. The final K—*keep your concentration*—is a learned skill. Insisting that the rigger operate the rigging for an established number of performances without an error before certification is one way of accomplishing this. One facility requires 100 consecutive perfect shows before issuing a competency certificate. If a rigger blows a cue on the 99th show, it's back to the beginning of the count for that crew member. This is a true test of keeping your concentration while running a show.

Glossary
Selected Bibliography

Glossary

act curtain. Also called a *front curtain* or *main curtain;* the curtain closest to the proscenium that opens and closes to expose the stage area to the audience.

apron. The area of the stage that is in front of the proscenium.

auditorium. The area where the audience is seated; also called the *house.*

a'vista. A scene change that occurs in full view of the audience.

batten. A steel pipe or wooden bar used to support scenery, curtains, and lights, usually suspended from the grid or roof structure on the lift or lead lines of a rigging set.

bridge. A movable steel structure suspended over the stage or audience area, usually used for suspending lighting instruments.

captured stage equipment. Machinery that is part of the structure of the building or is contained in a temporary stage floor, such as electromechanically or hydraulically driven wagons or turntables.

catching device. A protective shield that prevents the system operator from injury should a counterweight become dislodged and fall from the counterweight carriage.

catwalk. A steel structure over the stage, the audience area, or both, used by stage personnel to cross from one side to the other.

controlled stop. A timed deceleration of a moving device.

counterweight carriage. A metal frame that holds the counterweights used to balance the weight of flown scenery; also referred to as the *arbor, cradle,* or *carriage.*

counterweights. A system of variable weights used to counterbalance loads placed on battens that are moved vertically.

dead hung. Battens or similar equipment that is permanently supported from the grid and cannot be easily lowered to the stage floor.

deflecting device. Same as *catching device.*

drive damage. Any event that would impair, alter, or diminish the safe operation of the unit that contains the item.

expert. A person having extensive training and knowledge in the field of stage rigging and stage machinery.

fire curtain. A nonflammable curtain immediately behind the proscenium, contained in the smoke pocket, used to protect the audience from possible smoke and fire originating from the stage area.

fly. To move scenery or similar devices vertically on the stage.

fly gallery. A platform attached to the side wall of the stage house used to operate the rigging devices.

fly loft. The space above the grid and below the roof.

grid. A steel framework above the stage area that is used to support the rigging system; short for *gridiron*.

hard contact. A sudden or uncontrolled stop of the counterweight carriage caused by hitting the upper or lower limits of the system.

hemp system. A system of hemp (Manila fiber) ropes used for support to raise or lower scenery.

house. See *auditorium.*

loading gallery. A platform attached to the side walls of the stage house used for the loading or unloading of the counterweight carriages.

loft block. The pulleys or sheaves directly above the batten used to change the direction of the working lines from horizontal to vertical.

motorized rigging. A system of electric or hydraulic motors used to raise and lower battens or counterweight carriages.

mouse. (1) To wire the throat of a hook to prevent a cable or line from jumping out of the hook; (2) to interweave the barrel of a turnbuckle with wire to keep it from unscrewing; (3) placing wire or cotterpins through holes drilled in the endfittings of a turnbuckle.

orchestra lift. An elevator in the orchestra pit used to raise and lower the floor of the pit.

pin rail. A part of a hemp system consisting of a metal pipe or wooden rail attached to the fly gallery and fitted with removable steel or wooden pins used in tying off the working lines.

pit. A recessed area in front of the stage used principally by musicians; can also be covered and used as an extended forestage.

proper training. Training from a reputable school, college, university, venue, or IATSE local that has a formalized apprentice program.

proscenium. The wall between the stage and the audience containing the proscenium arch.

rigging. The general term describing systems used to raise, lower, or move the stage equipment overhead.

set. A unit of rigging consisting of the batten and all other support cables, sheaves, and mountings.

sheave. A grooved wheel in a block or pulley.

spreader plates. Movable steel plates on a counterweight arbor used to keep the arbor rods from spreading and the counterweights from falling out in case of a sudden stop.

stage house. That portion of a theatre building containing the stage area, fly loft, grid, and galleries.

supervisor. A person charged with the responsibility of directing the work of others and the safe operation of stage equipment.

technical stage equipment. A general term indicating the equipment or machinery used on a stage to support the movement of scenery, lighting equipment, and people.

thrust stage. An extension of the stage floor into the auditorium, allowing the audience to be seated on 3 sides.

traps. Sections of the stage floor that can be removed to access the understage area.

turntable. A rotating platform or portion of the stage floor.

wagon. A movable platform usually on casters or wheels.

well. The space between the beams on the grid over which the loft blocks are placed and the working lines to drop to the batten.

winch. A manual or power-operated device used to wind on cable to raise and lower stage equipment.

Selected Bibliography

Books

American Institute of Steel Construction. *Manual of Steel Construction Allowable Stress Design.* 9th ed. Chicago. 1989. Contains specific size information on all currently milled structural steel shapes, design and strength information, and mill practice. Good reference book. It is available by contacting the AISC at 400 N. Michigan Ave., Chicago, IL 60611.

American Iron and Steel Institute. *Wire Rope Sling Users Manual.* Washington, DC, 1990. See *Wire Rope Users Manual.*

————. *Wire Rope Users Manual.* Washington, DC, 1979. Good general information on wire rope and wire-rope slings. They are available through Strahm Printing and Mailing, 514 W. 26th St., Kansas City, MO 64108. 816-842-3351.

Ashley, Clifford W. *The Ashley Book of Knots.* Garden City, NY: Doubleday, 1944. The most complete book of knots available.

Barnes Group. *Fastener Facts.* Cleveland: Bowman Distribution, 1993. Excellent information on bolts and threaded fasteners. It is available by contacting Bowman Distribution, Barnes Group, Inc., 850 E. 72d St., Cleveland, OH 44103. 1-800-877-8800.

Bignon, Mario, and Guido Regazzoni. *The Morrow Guide to Knots.* Trans. Maria Piotrowska. New York: Quill Press, 1982. Excellent book on knot tying. Very easy to follow photographs.

Burris-Meyer, Harold, and Edward C. Cole. *Scenery for the Theatre*, 2d ed. Boston: Little, Brown, 1971. Excellent resource for traditional scenic applications.

Construction Safety Association of Ontario. *Rigging Manual.* 1975. Excellent information on construction rigging. Available by contacting the CSAO at 74 Victoria St., Toronto, Ontario, Canada M5C 2A5. 416-366-1501.

Ellis, J. Nigel. *Introduction to Fall Protection.* 2d ed. Des Plaines, IL: American Society for Safety Engineers, 1993. As the name implies, it is a good introduction to fall protection and the rigging required to set up safe systems. It is available by contacting the ASSE at 1800 E. Oakton St., Des Plaines, IL 60018.

Gillette, A. S. *Stage Scenery: Its Construction and Rigging.* 2d ed. New York: Harper & Row, 1972. Good schematics for solving rigging problems with traditional scenery.

Gordon, J. E. *The New Science of Strong Materials.* Princeton: Princeton University Press, 1976. Interesting discussion of the properties of structural materials. As with all of his books, it is fun to read.

———. *Structures, or Why Things Don't Fall Down.* Princeton: Princeton University Press, 1978. Excellent information on the effects of forces and reactions on structures and materials. Fun to read.

Graumont, Raoul, and John Hensel. *Splicing Wire and Fiber Rope.* Centerville, MD: Cornell Maritime Press, 1973. Good illustrations on splicing wire rope.

International Brotherhood of Electrical Workers. *Knot Tying and Rigging.* Washington, DC, 1986. Good information on block and tackle, gin pole, guy line, and other lineman rigging techniques. It is available from the IBEW, 1125 15th St., NW, Washington, DC 20005.

Jenson, Alfred, and Harry H. Chenoweth. *Statics and Strength of Materials.* Highstown, New J: McGraw-Hill, 1983. Good resource for more information on these subjects.

Long, John. *How to Rock Climb.* Evergreen, CO: Chockstone Press, 1989. Good source on climbing techniques, rappelling, and knots. It is available in mountain-climbing equipment stores and by contacting Chockstone Press at P. O. Box 3505, Evergreen, CO 80439.

Merry, Barbara. *The Splicing Handbook.* Camden, ME: International Marine Publishing Company, 1987. Covers splicing stranded, braided, and parallel-core fiber ropes. Good illustrations and directions.

Newberry, W. G. *Handbook for Riggers.* Self-published, Calgary, Alberta. 1967. Pocket handbook on construction rigging with good information on rigging components. It is available by contacting W. G. Newberry at P. O. Box 2999, Calgary, Alberta, Canada T2P 2M7.

Padgett, Allen, and Bruce Smith. *On Rope.* Huntsville, AL: National Speleological Society, 1987. Information on rope selection, knots, and techniques for climbing and descending rope. Available by contacting the NSS at Cave Ave., Huntsville, AL 35810. 205-852-1300.

Rossnagle, W. E., Lindley R. Higgins, and Joseph A. MacDonald. *Handbook of Rigging.* Highstown, N J: McGraw-Hill, 1988. Excellent reference on construction rigging, components, block and tackle, and friction factors.

Sammler, Ben, and Don Harvey, eds. *The Technical Brief Collection.* Department of Technical Design and Production, Yale

School of Drama. New Haven, CT 1992. Well-documented solutions to a number of specific rigging problems.

Wulpi, Donald J. *Understanding How Components Fail.* Metals Park, OH: American Society of Metals, 1985. Good explanations of component failure. Easy to understand without an engineering or mathematical background.

Catalogs

CM Lifting, Pulling, and Binding Products Manual. Columbus McKinnon Corporation, 140 John James Audobon Pkwy. Amherst, N Y 14228. 716-689-5400. Good information on chain design and inspection, shackles, and CM hardware.

Cordage Institute, Publications Department, 42 North St., Hingham, MA 02043. 617-749-1016. There are various publications available on fiber rope.

The Crosby Catalog. The Crosby Group, P.O. Box 3128, 2810 Dawson Rd., Tulsa, OK 74101. 918-834-4611. Excellent information on miscellaneous hardware and fittings.

Macwhyte Wire Rope Catalog G-18. Macwhyte Wire Rope Corporation, 2906 14th Ave. Kenosha, WI 53141. 414-654-5381. Excellent information about wire rope.

Jay O. Glerum has worked in theatre and the entertainment industry for forty years. During that time he has been a stagehand, designed scenery and lighting, taught technical theatre at several universities, consulted on numerous theatre and television studio projects, and worked as a systems designer for a major theatre equipment company. Glerum regularly teaches classes on stage rigging throughout the United States, Canada, and Europe. He currently is chairman of the Rigging and Stage Machinery Standards Committee of the United States Institute for Theatre Technology, a fellow of the Institute, and president of Jay O. Glerum & Associates, Inc., a firm specializing in consulting for the entertainment industry.